Imagining Church

Imagining Church

Seeing Hope
in a World of Change

GARY SHOCKLEY
AND KIM SHOCKLEY

THE
ALBAN
INSTITUTE

The Alban Institute
2121 Cooperative Way, Suite 100
Herndon, VA 20171

Scripture quotations noted NIV are from Holy Bible: New International Version, copyright © 1973, 1978, 1984. Used by permission of Zondervan Bible Publishers.

Scripture quotations noted NLT are from Holy Bible. New Living Translation, copyright © 1996, 2004 by Tyndale Charitable Trust. Used by permission of Tyndale House Publishers.

Scripture quotations noted NRSV are from the New Revised Standard Version of the Bible, copyright © 1989, Division of Christian Education of the National Council of Churches of Christ in the United States of America, and are used by permission.

Cover design by Tobias Becker, Bird Box Design.

Library of Congress Cataloging-in-Publication Data
Shockley, Gary A.
    Imagining church : seeing hope in a world of change / Gary A. Shockley and Kim Shockley.
        p. cm.
    Includes bibliographical references.
    ISBN 978-1-56699-373-9
    1. Church. I. Shockley, Kim. II. Title.
    BV600.3.S49 2008
    253—dc22

                                                    2008036683

            09   10   11   12   13   VP   5   4   3   2   1

Contents

Preface

∽

*T*hough we sat near each other in Abnormal Psychology and exchanged casual glances every now and then, the two of us didn't really "see" each other until that class had ended and we met up again at a denominational meeting intended for those considering a pathway toward ordained ministry. We reintroduced ourselves to each other, sat together at the end of the conference table, and didn't hear another word the presenter was saying. It was as though we were the only two people in the room.

From the start, the two of us shared a similar faith journey. We grew up in families that embraced the importance of the local church. Early on in our lives, we sensed a call to ministry. Kim sought to fulfill her calling through Christian education and Gary pursued ordained ministry. Except for two years (while we attended colleges six hours apart), we have been together for more than thirty years.

Over the past three decades we have served numerous churches in almost every conceivable setting; codirected leadership, marital, and spiritual retreats; copresented at denominational gatherings; planted two new churches; and raised two awesome sons. Now we can add to our list of cooperative endeavors the writing of a book. If you want to test the strength of any significant relationship try this!

What we present in this book is a culmination of our experiences—struggles, successes, and failures—of ministry in the local church. It clearly defines our personal vision for what we believe the church is called to be in this postmodern age where all the lines are blurred, everything familiar is challenged, and the need for effective, healthy churches has never been greater.

As we look out into this world of phenomenal change we continue to imagine what the church can be and in so doing we have hope. Join us!

Acknowledgments

∽

We are only as good as the people with whom we surround ourselves. We both wish to honor our parents—Ed and Barb Shultz and Richard and Alice Shockley—for getting us started on this fantastic voyage.

Kim wishes to acknowledge especially the impact Sharon Schwab and Dottie Walker have had on her personal and professional journey. Both women provided excellent mentoring and opportunities for stretching professionally. Gary wishes to acknowledge his pastor and mentor Robert Miller and seminary professor and friend Jerry Flora for expanding his vision of the church.

We are especially grateful for the excellent guidance and honesty of our editor Beth Gaede. Writing can be painful at times—sometimes Beth caused the sting and other times she provided the salve. For both we are grateful. Our appreciation also to Andrea Lee for the careful editing of our final manuscript. Her skills helped polish this diamond in the rough.

Finally, we honor the men and women in ministry with whom we have been and are pleased to call friends. To everyone who labors in ministry—keep the hope alive. The world is counting on us!

Introduction

❧

I sat in the family room near the big bay window as I worked on another pencil sketch. I squirmed atop the mohair chaise lounge that itched against my bare back. Leaning forward helped to alleviate the discomfort but made it more difficult to hold the paper on my lap. I would lean back again with my feet perched on the edge of the couch, creating a makeshift easel with my knees until the skin on my back began to crawl once more. Most of the other eight-year-old boys I knew were outside riding bikes or playing games. I was content to rock back and forth on that itchy old piece of furniture, capturing the images floating in my head and transferring them to paper. I would run to my parents to unveil my masterpieces. They loved everything I showed them, which only fueled my desire to draw all the more.

That same year someone outside the family discovered this budding Picasso. One of my mother's friends dropped by for afternoon coffee as I busied myself at the kitchen table with a paint-by-number kit of a sailboat cast against a choppy sea. Never much for following directions, I ignored the little numbers inside each squiggly space and opted instead to paint it the way I saw it in my head. It was messy and, I would have to say, not my best work, but my mother's friend, an art teacher, was impressed enough to convince my parents to sign me up for painting lessons. Once a week for a year I toted my art supplies three blocks to her basement studio where, with a half dozen other students, I learned the fine art of oil painting. No numbers or squiggly lines to ignore, just a blank canvas waiting to be touched by genius. I loved those lessons. Forty years later, most of the paintings from this early period still hang in the homes of my relatives across the country. The sailboat painting adorns the wall of my ninety-one-year-old grandmother's room at a nursing home. Adjacent to it hangs my third oil painting—a rendering of long-stemmed daisies in a brass pitcher. Of all the things my Nana took from her home to bring to this place, she included my paintings. I am thrilled to know they continue to bring her joy. Though I haven't worked in oils since that time, I can still close my eyes and imagine the pungent smell of linseed oil and paint thinner. When I completed my lessons and began painting at home, I discovered, with my parents' help, the mediums of watercolor and acrylic. They were less smelly and messy and didn't take nearly as long to dry, which meant I could paint faster.

I think most people can identify certain activities that help them experience the nearness of God—reading, walking along a wooded path, working a craft, meandering on the beach, serving a neighbor in need, volunteering to help the homeless, golfing on a beautiful spring morning, biking, studying Scripture, toiling in the garden, practicing spiritual disciplines, or even writing a book—these things have the potential to help us become more open to the simple presence of God. Almost any kind of artistic endeavor does that for me. It has since I was very young.

As far back as I can remember, I never had any doubt that God existed, was watching over me, loved me, and wanted me to do what was right. I am not sure it was any more complex than that. Faith was a simple, unquestioned part of my life. It seemed to become more complicated when I entered college as a religion major and then moved on to seminary to experience more heady things like higher criticism, apologetics, church dogma, and deep theological constructs. All of this capped off by six semesters of Greek and Hebrew. While these were all incredibly worthwhile experiences, somehow in the midst of them God seemed to become more distant from me. No longer a simple presence in my life, God became something to be analyzed, intellectualized, and argued over. God went from being some*one* I related to, in a very childlike manner to be sure, to some*thing* I thought about, picked apart, and scrutinized in a very impersonal way. I understand that all this higher learning was a necessary part of my training to be a pastor and that it was helping me think more critically about God, the church, the world, and myself. But the childlike and more heartfelt images I had of God seemed to be fading away from me, and I found that distressing. I can see now that these educational experiences were broadening the images I previously had of God and simultaneously the images I had of myself. I was learning how much imagination is a key part of spiritual growth and maturation.

From the Latin *imago*, to imagine means to create a mental image of something that isn't there. Seeing something and duplicating it on paper or canvas has always been easy for me as an artist. For this reason I favor landscapes and seascapes over more contemporary abstract forms of art. But, as I have been trying to stretch myself artistically these past few years, my paintings are taking on a much more imaginative style. The colors I am choosing are much more vibrant. I am adding things that weren't in the photos I have taken of my subject matter and changing things to suit how I would like them to be. I am exercising more of my imagination.

Imagination is one of the great gifts bestowed on us by our Creator. We are by nature imaginative people. When we sit at our favorite restaurant and peruse the menu, we look at the list of entrees, read some of the ingredients and imagine how delightful the dish will be. Our mouths may even begin to water in anticipation. As we wake up in the morning and prepare for the day, we may find ourselves imagining how we are going to lead an important meeting, work through a conflict with a coworker, or ask the boss for a promotion. When we are away from our spouses, children, or friends for any length of time, we may find ourselves imagining the kinds of things we might do when we are reunited to express how much we love them.

I recently finished a book where the author writes about spiritual friendships and neighborliness. I found myself imagining the kind of neighbor I would like to be to the people living around us. We moved into this community a little less than a year ago and it has been difficult getting to know folks because we all live such busy lives. A quick hello is the sorry extent of most of our conversations. Anyway, I have been imagining the kind of neighbor I would really like to be—one who takes a real interest in others beyond saying hello, who takes the time to get to know them by their first name, who is available to help them when they need it. I shared this with Kim a few nights ago and expressed it as something I have been praying about. Today an opportunity came to exercise my imagination into action. The neighbors who rent the home immediately behind ours got way behind in mowing their lawn. This is our rainy season in central Florida and we have to mow our lawns twice a week to keep up with the growth. For whatever reason, our neighbors haven't mowed their lawn in well over a month. The grass was almost four feet tall. I began to think that the house was empty and that was the reason for the neglect. But at lunchtime today Kim noticed our neighbor struggling to get a lawnmower through his yard. He would take two steps and the mower would choke and die. Pulling the clumped grass from under the mower he would start it up once more, take two steps, and it would die again. My son Jake and I went over to him and offered our help. I told him Jake was trying to save money for a car and would be glad to mow his lawn on a regular basis for a very reasonable fee. He hired Jake to help him and I decided to assist them with our mower. In less than an hour we had his lawn under control again. Our neighbor was extremely grateful. It wasn't until we were finished and I was soaking in our pool that it hit me—I had become the neighbor I imagined myself to be.

When we can imagine—form a mental image of something that is not there—and work toward making it become a reality we are cocreators with God. The new church Kim and I are helping our denomination start will begin meeting for weekly worship in just a few months. I find myself in quieter moments closing my eyes and imagining how the people who come on Sunday mornings to worship will relate to each other. I imagine them milling around the room greeting each other with hugs and handshakes. I imagine a room full of people who are open, welcoming, and accepting of everyone. No one is sitting by himself or herself or standing alone in a corner. I hear lots of laughter and I see bright genuine smiles. I see and hear authentic love in action. I am using the gift of imagination to form a strong mental image of something that does not yet exist. I know the power of that imagination will color how I and members of my staff will plan worship, establish an environment with lighting and music, work on the flow of the room, and even decide what kinds of refreshments we will serve. Imagination is a godly and powerful thing.

For me to effectively serve God in and through the church requires abundant imagination and creativity. I am grateful, by God's grace, to know that the fruitfulness of my ministry does not depend on my having all the resources and wherewithal to do anything significant for God. At best I am called to step into the flow of God's activity and, using the gifts he has given me, cooperate in his work. For me this necessarily includes regular occasions for quiet prayer when I take time to imagine how God is working and see myself in partnership with him.

Kim and I had a seminary professor, Dr. Munson, who used to say of preaching and teaching, "If you can't see it, neither will anyone else." Until I imagine, until I have a picture in mind of what I believe the church is and ought to be, it will be darn near impossible for me to help anyone else imagine church. If I can't see it, neither will they.

Imagining church, we believe, is a shared experience. I used to think that my role as a pastoral leader was to discern God's vision, God's imagination of the church, and tender it to everyone else. People, I believed, would be waiting for me to come down whatever mountain I had been on to deliver *the* word from God. Eyes popping, mouths salivating, hearts pounding, they would be awash in anticipation for *the* picture of what God imagines for us. Silly me!

Our new congregation was only one year into its journey when I decided to gather our leaders for a Saturday morning event designed to cast *my* vision for the church. My intent was to indoctrinate this first tier of leadership in the ways of my carefully thought-out five-year plan for ministry. "They're going to be so impressed with this!" I remember thinking to myself. "This will convince the yet unconvinced that this is a worthy project to invest themselves in." I had neatly ordered notebooks for each partici- pant, replete with slick four-color inserts in the front. I arranged the tables in the room so they formed a giant U shape. I would stand in the opening of the U so as to see and be seen by each person. The notebooks were placed neatly on the tables alongside a brand new pen. Every table had a pitcher of water and a bowl of assorted candies. It was a professional setup! Gradually people straggled in and found their seats. At exactly ten o'clock I greeted the group and opened with prayer. A few latecomers arrived, fill- ing in the holes around the tables. I stopped and greeted the group again. Soon two more people arrived. I paused while they found their seats. Feeling a little flustered by this staggered start I took a long, deep breath and began again. I invited everyone to open the notebooks and follow along as I reviewed each section, beginning with our vision statement. I asked everyone to read it aloud with me. They did and without much energy. I encouraged them to do it again with a little more enthusiasm. They obliged. I pressed on dissecting the statement phrase by phrase for added empha- sis, offering quick commentary about why I felt each phrase was particularly important. They weren't seeing it and I could see they weren't seeing it. I found myself kicking into salesman mode es- pousing all the reasons I felt it was a good vision and right for our church. They didn't seem to be buying it. I tried harder—which for an extroverted feeler means—talk about it more and more and more until they are convinced. They weren't. I eventually stopped to ask for questions. There were none. I had explained the vision so thoroughly that in so doing had sucked all the life completely out of it. In the end the group remained uninspired and, honestly, I was beginning to feel that way too.

What went wrong? In retrospect probably a lot of things. For starters I didn't give people time to introduce themselves to each other. I was so focused on giving them the right information that I neglected to think about how they might be formed relation- ally by this experience. My wife would tell me that my presentation style was so heavily auditory that I ignored the needs of the more visual and kinesthetic-style learners. Another mistake I tend to make, even now when I lead discussions, is I answer questions that haven't even been asked. In short, information overload. But I think the real crux of the problem was simply this—I never invited them to share whatever God-inspired picture *they* had of our church. Because my approach didn't appeal to their prayerful and playful imaginations, they were left to consider only my monochromatic snapshot of the church.

Sadly, this kind of encounter gets repeated too often in our churches. I could say that church leaders tend to the business of the church much in the same way the corporations some of our members belong to care for their business. The truth is that many of these "secular" businesses conduct themselves with far more imagination and creativity than our churches. And we are the ones who claim relationship with the Master Designer, Chief Architect, and Greatest Creator there ever was or ever will be!

Through the pages of this book, Kim and I won't be asking you to color inside the lines we have drawn or buy into *our* ideas of what the church is or should be. We will invite you to use your imagination to consider how God is at work in your present ministry context and open yourself anew to the Spirit of God—the Divine Artist—who is ready to fuel your desire to be the creative artist you are meant to be for the sake of the church. You won't have to squirm on a mohair couch or form an easel with your knees. The tools you need are already in your head and heart. So, let's begin!

⤚

CHAPTER 1

The Constant Waves
of Change

D o you remember the first globe you ever owned? If you are a baby boomer like Kim and me, or older, you will remember when we were in school how globes were fairly reliable sources of geographical information. I had one that was illuminated from the inside, creating an eerie yellow glow to my bedroom. I could refer back to my lighted globe most of my school years, knowing it would be a trustworthy source of information. I read somewhere that a globe nowadays is only accurate for about six months. The names and boundaries of countries around the world change that often.

While the geographical changes in our world during the past few decades have been astounding, they haven't personally affected most of us like the ones we have seen, for example, in the realms of technology. What was technology like when you graduated from high school or started your first job? I remember that my first church office had a beige rotary dial telephone, a feisty hand-cranked mimeograph machine that tended to spit black ink everywhere, a manual typewriter missing the *q* key (I substituted with the *g*), and a Rolodex complete with real paper cards for each of my church contacts. Computers weren't available to the general public because no one had a room large enough to contain one. When I needed to research something for a sermon, I went to the library and spent hours thumbing through dusty books. If I needed to send a note to someone, I used the good old U.S. Postal Service. When it came to marketing the ministries of the church, I had to rely mostly on word of mouth, homemade posters displayed in storefront windows, and, since we were fortunate enough to have one, a cleverly worded lighted sign out front. Ah, the good old days.

As I am sitting in one of my favorite booksellers working on this chapter, I am typing on a small laptop computer using a wireless mouse. I have Internet access, thanks to wireless technology. My PDA is open in front of me so that I can hear the alarm, which I set to remind myself of my next meeting this afternoon. My cell phone, which has a digital camera, also sports an MP3 player and a kickin' set of earbuds currently pumping in the band Chicago's greatest hits. Who could have imagined tools like these would someday be in the hands of ministers like me? I can only imagine what will be in store for us in the next ten years!

Cultural Waves of Change

Sociologists tell us that over the past several centuries a series of powerful waves of cultural change have crashed upon us. These movements have thrown, and will continue to throw, us personally and collectively off balance until we acknowledge and make the necessary adjustments to accommodate them. During the earlier days of my pastoral experience, I was naively unaware of just how much these waves would affect my personal and professional life and even the churches I have been called to serve.

Having grown up in a fairly typical small town community in the 1950s and '60s, I inherited a healthy respect for both God and country. In fact, thanks especially to my mother, these two allegiances were inseparable for me. I remember sitting beside her on my bed learning some of the old hymns of the faith *and* songs of our country. Mom taught me the rosary (she was a former Catholic) *and* the pledge to the flag. For the Shockleys to be good Christians meant also being patriotic citizens and vice versa.

The church occupied a central place in our lives and in the communal life of Milton, Delaware. What the church did and what the church said mattered to the citizens of our town. No person or business knowingly did anything that would even appear to compete with or undermine the work of our church. Like most of the people of our town, our family went to worship nearly every Sunday. I can close my eyes and still picture exactly where I sat in the sanctuary with my three siblings. We were bookended by my mom and dad in the fourth row on the right side. Dad sat nearest to the aisle. I always figured he took that position to expedite our quick escape after the benediction. There was never any doubt what the Shockleys would be doing on Sunday mornings. We would clean up, dress up, and drive up to the small brownstone St. John's Episcopal Church in Milton, Delaware, and after worship make the five-mile trip to my grandparents' home across town for Sunday dinner. Except for illness or a stray hurricane, this was our weekly routine.

Learning Church

At the ripe old age of eighteen I began serving a church as a part-time student pastor. "Student pastorates," as they are called, are still generally available for people attending seminary in the United Methodist Church, though it was, and still is, very rare for someone so young to serve a church in his or her first year of college. My well-intentioned and often misguided attempts at filling that holy role grew out of the relationships I had with my two earliest pastoral role models—Father Mosby and Reverend Miller.

Father Mosby, rector of St. John's Episcopal Church, was the very first pastor I remember. Though probably only in his early forties at the time, Father Mosby seemed ancient to me. Average in height with a stocky build, he had a stern face topped with thick, wavy brown hair. The black suits and black shirts he wore, complete with white-banded collars around his neck, accentuated the severity of his demeanor. No matter where I saw him in town, that is how Father Mosby dressed. I often wondered if he mowed the lawn or tinkered in the garage dressed like that. Father Mosby went about the tasks of preaching, sharing the sacraments, and leading us through worship with a definite sense of solemnity and rote. It has only been a few years since Father Mosby, now probably in his early eighties, fully retired from that little church in Milton. Talk about staying power. And I have been told by relatives who still attend there that very little changed in the life of the church throughout his tenure.

We moved from Delaware to New Jersey when I was nine and for the next five years became inactive in the church. Motivated by the prospects of homemade cookies and Kool-Aid, my brother and I would occasionally meander down to one of the churches in town. If the cookies were good, we would go back. Sadly, we didn't visit too many churches a second time. During our stint in New Jersey, our family never connected with a local church. I guess we were so steeped in our familiar expression of religion at St. John's Church we couldn't imagine ourselves anywhere else, but that all changed for me when we moved again, to central Pennsylvania.

I was the first to visit Mount Calvary United Methodist Church only a quarter mile from our house. One of the guys who befriended me at school was a member of their youth fellowship. Reverend Robert Miller was pastor of the church. Like Father Mosby, he dressed in black with a white-banded collar. Average in height with thick white hair, Reverend Miller was a jovial man with ample charisma and charm. His preaching was engaging and his personal warmth winsome. Reverend Miller was the second pastor of Mount Calvary, which had begun in a barn five years before his appointment. The fairly new church mirrored its age with lots of young families. It was under Reverend Miller's leadership that I declared my calling to pastoral ministry. He was a sly man! I remember taking a trip to the office supply store one Saturday morning to help him carry cartons of paper back to his office. On the way home he turned to me with an impish grin that betrayed a certain devilishness and asked, "Gary, when are you going to get on with serving the Lord? When you get around to it?" I was caught off guard by the abruptness of his question and immediately turned bright red. Trying to quickly recover from blushing, I answered, "Yeah, when I get around to it!" We both chuckled. Reaching into his pocket, he retrieved a wooden button about two inches in diameter. Handing it to me he said, "So, there you are." I looked down at the writing on the button. In big bold blue letters it read, "Round Tuit" and, underneath in smaller print, "I will serve the Lord when I get a round tuit." I still keep this treasure in my jewelry box.

I think it was about two years later when I visited Reverend Miller in his office to ask him what it felt like to be called into ordained ministry. For well over a year I sensed God had been up to something in my life. Every sermon I heard seemed to be pointing me toward some kind of professional ministry. One Sunday after worship, I asked Reverend Miller, "Why are you directing your sermons at me? And what do you want me to do?" He assured me that he wasn't intentionally aiming his messages in my direction. He added that it might just be the work of God's Spirit in my life. He encouraged me to think and pray about that. Over the next several months, people would stop me in church and ask, "Have you ever thought about going into the ministry? I think you'd be a great pastor." Reverend Miller denied any conspiracy on his part but I always wondered.

During the four years of my student pastorate, Reverend Miller was always there to check on me and encourage my work. Not long after my ordination, Reverend Miller died of a heart attack. After the funeral his family removed the cross he had always worn in ministry and placed it around my neck. Because I was the only person to become an ordained pastor under his leadership, his family said he considered me the only jewel he would have in his crown in heaven.

I learned most of what I understood about the church and how it engages culture from Father Mosby and Reverend Miller. I learned to see the church and the world through their eyes.

Each in his own way had birthed into reality what they themselves imagined the church to be—a faith community that occupied a central place in society. It was their experience that the church sat in the midst of a culture that readily respected it and supported its services and events. With little or nothing to compete against its activities—Sunday worship, Wednesday night Bible study, youth fellowship, women's circle, and the like—the church only needed to post the times of these events in its bulletin or on its outdoor signs and simply wait for people to show up. And they did. The idea of promoting the church the way many of us attempt to do it today would have seemed ridiculous to Father Mosby and Reverend Miller. It wasn't necessary because the church, as a respected entity and institution, was still valued and supported by the majority of our culture.

The Rising and Receding Wave of Christendom

Father Mosby, Reverend Miller, and I began our ministries in the overlapping cultural eras commonly known as Christendom and modernity. Historians point to the advent of Christendom in the fourth century AD, when in 313 Emperor Constantine and Licinius, who married Constantine's sister Constantia, agreed to end the persecution of Christians throughout the Roman Empire. A portion of the edict Constantine and Licinius enacted, translated into English, read: "When I, Constantine Augustus, as well as I, Licinius Augustus, fortunately met near Mediolanurn (Milan), and were considering everything that pertained to the public welfare and security, we thought, among other things which we saw would be for the good of many, those regulations pertaining to the reverence of the Divinity ought certainly to be made first, so that we might grant to the Christians and others full authority to observe the religion which each preferred."[1]

Constantine was a powerful general preparing for battle against his rival for the imperial throne when, as legend has it, he stopped to consider which gods he should pray to for guidance and help. He looked up to the sky and saw the sign of the cross bearing the words, "Conquer by this." He marched under this sign and was consequently victorious in battle. Though never going so far as to declare it the official religion of the empire, he ended three centuries of persecution against the cult known as Christianity.[2]

Imagine the huge shift this caused for the state since, prior to this, it had openly persecuted Christians and the church. The shift was even more significant for the church as it had to adjust from being on the outside of things to now being legitimized by the government and accepted by the masses. As Christianity's roots deepened, the Roman Empire was divided into parishes or geographical areas serviced by a local church and its appointed priest. People automatically became members of whatever parish church they lived near. The purpose of the church was to serve the people around it. In turn the people of the parish were responsible for supporting and maintaining the church. The parish served the people and the people served the parish. Sound familiar? Essentially, since the fourth century the church has occupied a place of prominence and privilege in the Western world.

Christendom Comes to America

The founders of the United States, in drafting the Declaration of Independence, sought to guard against the creation of state-sponsored religion. Thomas Jefferson, given the task of writing the Declaration of Independence, stressed that the power of the government is derived from the governed and not from kings ruling by the authority of God. In 1797, a treaty written under the presidency of George Washington and signed under the presidency of John Adams—stated: "The Government of the United States of America is not, in any sense, founded on the Christian religion."[3] Whether it is true that Jefferson or the other signers of the Declaration of Independence were Christian (and there is great debate about that, depending on whom you read), the fact was that most of the early settlers of this new country held to a predominately Judeo-Christian belief system, so the church received unofficial support and endorsement by most facets of society. This was still true when I was growing up. Sunday-closing laws, or "blue laws," prohibited certain activities on Sunday.

Blue laws date back to the colonial period, starting with a 1610 law that required the citizens of Jamestown to keep the Sabbath day holy.[4] The blue laws movement eventually brought an increase in the level of restrictions placed on public and private conduct on Sundays, including bans on all unnecessary work. Church groups and some merchants' associations supported these measures, arguing that society would benefit greatly if citizens were required to take a day of rest. I think they had something there. In some states like Virginia, people were arrested and fined for things like selling soda pop or peanuts and for showing movies or operating public swimming pools on Sundays.

Due in large part to the proliferation of Sunday-closing or blue laws during the first two centuries after U.S. independence, the church enjoyed a place of prominence in U.S. society. When moral or ethical debate arose, people instinctively turned to the church for guidance. Clergy were recognized among the most educated, articulate, and respected sources of personal and communal authority. Local churches, like St. John's Episcopal Church in Milton, had respected influence over their communities, and the larger the church, the greater influence it had. In the Christendom era, people came *to* the church that was closest to them.

Back in the 1960s our Little League teams practiced and played games every day *but* Sunday. The theater, pool hall, my grandfather's gas station, Norma Jean's Sub Shop, Welch's Jewelers, Sam Shapiro's Clothing Store, and the Scrapple plant—all closed on Sundays—even though half of these businesses were owned and operated by Jewish families. We never questioned it. It was just the way it was, out of deference to the church.

Is There Room for a Church?

Blue laws are long gone and now the stores are as busy, and sometimes busier, on Sundays as they are the rest of the week, evidence that our culture no longer caters to the needs and desires of any particular established faith community. Furthermore, the diminishing acquiescence of our culture toward faith communities is indicated by the difficulty many of these communities face trying to buy land, expand their facilities, or even remain on their own properties.

As local governments make way for malls and new housing developments touted to promote a sense of community, they are increasingly seizing churches or synagogues to secure land for such projects. As reported by Gannett News Service, "Government officials are increasingly insensitive or even hostile to houses of worship, passing ordinances excluding them from various neighborhoods or restricting their ability to expand."[5] Cited in the report are examples like Cottonwood Christian Center in Los Alamitos, California, which spent several years fighting the city's attempt to take the land the congregation had purchased to build a larger place of worship and sell it to Costco Corporation for their new store. With no end of litigation in sight, the case was finally settled when the church agreed to build on another piece of property in the same area. St. Luke's Pentecostal Church in North Hempstead, New York, started in a rented basement and, after years of sacrifice and struggle, was able to buy a piece of property on which to build their church. Through a series of complicated measures, the city managed to condemn the property for private retail development. The church fought the city's decision only to lose its case—and its land—in 2002.

Such confiscations are not isolated to Christian and Jewish communities of faith. In East St. Louis, Illinois, the Masjid Al-Muhajirum Mosque purchased land to build their place of worship. But a group of developers wanted the land for a residential complex. When the mosque wouldn't sell, the developers persuaded the government's development authority to condemn the land. In 1999 the government agreed to the developer's request, arguing that doing so was a valid "public use" because the land was blighted. The Muslims won in the trial court but lost on appeal. In 2001 the developers got the land.

As a church planter, I have faced my share of challenges when trying to buy land for the two churches I have started for our denomination. For nearly five years our sponsoring church has been working to buy land in a massive planned community in western Orange County, Florida, called Horizon West. When the development of Horizon West is completed, somewhere between sixty and eighty thousand new residents will live in seven villages surrounding a town center. Each village will have its own elementary school, shops, and community centers. A network of streets will connect these villages so that one could easily walk from one to the other. Each home is to have a porch out front to encourage a sense of community and driveways out back to minimize congestion on the streets. Because we are seeking to plant our church in this new mission field, I have personally met with the developers, county commissioners, and local zoning and planning boards to learn everything I can about the area and ascertain how and where our congregation might buy land for our new church. What I have learned is this: every provision has been made to include stores, fitness centers, community centers, parks and recreational areas in the master plan of Horizon West, but there isn't one square inch intentionally allocated for places of worship. Not one. When I have asked, "Is there room for a church?" as I have on numerous occasions, I get a great many excuses but no explanations.

Having been steeped in a Christendom cultural mind-set, I found this omission strange. No place for a church? How crazy is that? But, as I am beginning to realize, it is just another example of how much things have changed in my relatively brief life. And I now find myself thinking, why *would* they make special provisions for the "church" when every other faith expression I know of is out here too? Would I be content to see land set aside for a Shinto shrine or a Hindu temple? What right do I have to expect special treatment just because I am a Christian pastor planting a new congregation? In a Christendom culture, the church could just assume its place in the community. But we are no longer living in that culture. We are now living in a foreign land, and quite frankly many of us who have inherited leadership in the church don't particularly like or understand it. To be sure, vestiges of Christendom are still alive and well among us, but they seem oddly out of place. For example, political leaders and witnesses in court are sworn in as they place their hand on a Bible, chaplains lead sessions of Congress in prayer, and alcohol sales are banned on Sunday in some communities.

The Waves of Modernity and Postmodernity

Overlapping the remaining and yet waning influences of Christendom, another era referred to as the modern era or simply modernity emerged. Some suggest modernity appeared at the time of the philosopher Friedrich Nietzsche in the late nineteenth century or, as others suggest, in the last half of the twentieth century. It is important to note here that some writers use *modern* to mean post-Renaissance. More important than the dating of this era is modernity's impact on our culture.

In his "It's a Whole New World: An Online Course on Church and Culture in a New Time," United Church of Christ pastor and author Anthony B. Robinson describes modernity in terms of its "Big Five" hallmark values: reason, optimism, universality, objectivity, and "the grand story." Robinson writes, "Modernity held that reason and rational thought are the primary human faculties and the keys to gaining control over life and ridding the world of pernicious superstitions."[6] In other words, proponents of modernity expected their "modern" views about how the world works to counter the silly superstitions they felt religion promoted and that the things plaguing society—mostly ignorance, greed, and poverty—could be solved by science, education, and technology, *not* religion.

With its emphasis on objectivity, analysis, scientific discovery, and cogent criticism, modernity attempted to strip away any sense of the mystery and personal experience of religion by explaining away things of faith by objective scientific analysis.

Finally, modernity was powered by a big story, a metanarrative promising us moderns a coming age of personal prosperity and plenty and, for the United States, a place of increasing prominence in the world. With the help of reason, science, and technology, modernity promised that a new world of progress and prosperity was just around the corner and that as modern people we would become masters of our own destiny. The overlapping waves of Christendom and modernity are still present in our culture. As a church, we continue to be deeply influenced by them.

Sometime around the late 1990s yet another wave emerged, called postmodernity. Unlike moderns, who looked to science and reason for the answers to life's questions (while simultaneously explaining away mystery), postmoderns tend to be more aware of and open to things like intuition, emotional intelligence, embodied knowledge, and mystery. Thinking we have drunk too heavily at the well of reason, postmoderns want to explore life's questions *while experiencing* transcendence.

On their website, church consultants Easum, Bandy, and Associates offer this quick comparison between modernity and postmodernity.[7]

Modern	Postmodern
intellect, teaching, know	spirit, experience, sense
either/or	both/and/also
prove it to me	show it to me
institutional	organic
build churches	build the Kingdom

Many postmoderns would agree that through science and technology humans have gained control over some aspects of the world around us—for example, by building power plants that produce cheap and plentiful energy—but we have in the process destroyed nature and endangered creatures to the point of near extinction. While modern modes of transportation, for example, enable people to get around much faster and more efficiently, the resulting fossil fuel emissions are potentially raising the temperature of our planet to a point that threatens the well-being of our environment. When it comes to issues of faith, my experience has been that, like moderns, postmoderns enjoy intellectual debate and readily explore the facts of their own faith systems but, unlike moderns, are less likely to conclude with any definitive sense their way is *the* way. Postmoderns tend to be more open and tolerant of others who are on divergent spiritual pathways.

The Impact of Change on the Church's Ministries

Looking back nearly twenty-five years to the time of my college and seminary training, I see how much of it was built on a kind of hybrid Christendom/modernity model. I learned that one of the primary tasks I had as a Christendom-influenced pastor was to care for the people of *my* parish, which was a more tightly identified geographical area around the church building. When I first started in ministry, practices such as regularly visiting people in their homes, frequently stopping by the hospital to call on the sick, and dropping by the homes of visitors to the church were a given. Today only the oldest members of the church might expect a visit from me (and many of them are now too busy to entertain their pastor). Younger families do not have this expectation of me and, because a number of couples work outside of the home, it would be a major inconvenience for them. Because most surgeries are now done on an outpatient basis and hospital stays tend to be very short term, I make more phone calls than personal visits to follow up on the sick. I gave up doing the cookie drop at the homes of newcomers when members of my church (who had invited these new folks) informed me that it made their nonchurched friends uncomfortable.

While the assumptions of Christendom shaped the way I related to people in the early years of my parish ministry, I gradually came to see that my preaching and teaching were products of a more modern worldview. In the more modernistic classes I had in seminary, I learned how to pick apart the critical components of Scripture and my own Christian faith and then reconstruct it all in a very reasonable and rational way. Preaching was the way we modern clergy educated our congregations, assumed to already *be* mostly Christian, in the ways of our faith. Bible studies focused more critically on things like authorship, history, social-cultural context, and meaning filtered through our particular denominational theological lenses. Less emphasis was given to how we might live out the principles and lessons of a given passage in the context of our daily lives.

I could continue doing the things I was trained to do thirty years ago as a young pastor. But because the world around me has changed so much, the ways I meet and minister to the people around me need to change as well. I cannot assume that what worked thirty, ten, or even five years ago will necessarily work today. The need to study and then prepare myself, and the church I am serving, for the waves of change that keep coming never ends.

Imagining the Church in a Postmodern Culture

Planting another new church in our postmodern culture is challenging me in so many ways. My preaching, for example, has had to shift away from mere fact sharing to storytelling; from unloading information to uploading inspiration; from perpetuating one particular style or mode of worship to creating the kinds of environments where people can *encounter* God in a much more personal way. No longer able to assume that everyone in worship is necessarily Christian, I have to take time to explain what we are doing in the service and why. The music in worship at Hope-Spring would be considered more postmodern in style and is led by a praise band with guitar, drums, and keyboard rather than an organ and a choir. Where the intent of many of the church's traditional hymns was to convey doctrine and theology (a more modern goal), the songs we sing are intended mostly to invite people to express love, praise, and thanksgiving to God. We also incorporate more contemplative elements in worship, including the sacraments of communion and baptism, helping to create the space people need to open their hearts to the presence of God in quieter, more reflective, less rigidly structured ways.

Some people still deeply engrained in a Christendom/modern mind-set and looking for more predictable patterns of worship with a three-point, apologetic-style sermon might be confused and uncomfortable with what we are doing. But generally when I take time to explain that the church is trying to reach a new culture—one that seems very foreign—with elements of worship and ministry practices that are less familiar to many of us, they tend to become fairly supportive.

Later on Kim and I will present how the changing waves of post-Christendom, modernity, and postmodernity necessarily require the church to change the way it engages in evangelism. To reach a postmodern world requires us to think differently about ourselves *and* our communities. I remember meeting Anna at a church planting conference held near Orlando two years ago. Anna was a member of a very progressive contemporary church that had just a few years before relocated from a small white-framed church building that housed what she defined as a very traditional approach to ministry. The church bought land and constructed a modern facility on it, complete with a stage and every techno-gizmo you can imagine. When I met her, Anna was eighty-three. She was standing at the doorway leading into the worship space welcoming people to another conference worship event sponsored by her church. Loud, and I mean really *loud*, music was blasting from the stage. Now I am used to fairly up-tempo contemporary music in worship, but these sounds were a bit too much for me. Anna was dutifully at her post each day of the three-day event.

Curiosity finally got the best of me, and during one of the breaks I took Anna aside and asked her, "Is this the kind of music you have in worship every Sunday?" She nodded yes. "And are there other seniors in your church like you who attend worship every week?" She nodded yes again. "Please forgive me if this sounds insensitive but how does this appeal to someone your age?" Anna replied, smiling broadly, "This really isn't about me, is it? You need to know we were a dying church. I represented the average age of those attending. We knew if we were going to survive we'd better get busy doing what we're supposed to be doing—reaching people for the Lord. Five years ago we decided to sell our building and land and use the money to build a facility that would help us reach the young families who don't go to church. We knew we needed to do music and worship differently if we were going to reach them. Our services are now packed every week. I don't like the music much. But I remind myself that this isn't about me." What a generous spirit! Anna was able, along with others from her struggling church, to ride the wave of change and imagine a new way of being church in her community.

Reimagining Church

The overlapping waves of post-Christendom, modernity and postmodernity have left many of us in the church feeling a little disoriented. Whether I like it or not, mainline Protestant churches, like the ones I have served for over thirty years, can no longer assume the prominence or power they once enjoyed. In our current culture, my role as pastor is not as clear to me as it used to be.

The American soil I live on is now infused with many different cultures and faiths—Christianity, Judaism, Islam, Hinduism, Buddhism, New Age, and Mormonism, to name a few, as well as no religious faith at all. And in each of these religious—or nonreligious—traditions, dozens of expressions branch off in different directions. This is so evident here in central Florida. As a world destination, central Florida is home to people from all over the globe. Having moved here from a predominantly white suburban community in western Pennsylvania, I was surprised to find that in the fairly new suburban neighborhood where we live, we are the only Anglo family on the block. When the kids line up for school at the bus stop across the street from our house, not one Anglo child is among them. We have such a diverse mix of people living around us. When Kim and I take the dog for an evening walk, we encounter foreign dialects, unfamiliar religious icons, and assorted aromas pouring out of ovens and grills. We have learned to appreciate and embrace the diversity around us. But we are alarmed by the number of people we meet, mostly Christian, who have not. We have heard some of them say out loud, "*They* should speak English if they're going to live in *our* country!" and "Why aren't *they* coming to *our* church?"

For congregational leaders so strongly influenced by Christendom and modernity, the reimagining process might begin by acknowledging that things *have* changed in the world around us—that the church *is* in a much different place than perhaps we would like it to be, that the world *has* moved beyond us, and *we* must find a new way to incarnate the presence of the Divine in the world again. We can no longer sit around waiting and hoping for things to return to the way they used to be. We are called by God to imagine church, and ourselves as leaders in the church, in a new and exciting way.

Most of the mainline Protestant churches with which I was familiar back in the 1950s and '60s were vital, successful, growing, socially dynamic places. They effectively remained connected to the people in their neighborhoods. Studies like those conducted by researcher Diana Butler Bass, which she explores in her book *The Practicing Congregation: Imagining a New Old Church*, point out that many of these same churches continue to be vibrant communities of faith only because they have learned to effectively navigate the waves of cultural change that have affected them.

As church consultants who have spent considerable time working with declining and dying congregations, Kim and I have seen firsthand how churches that fail to find new ways to ride the ever-rippling waves of change tend to be overcome by them. Having lost the ability to reimagine themselves, such congregations dwindle in attendance, experience a decrease in financial support, and drift away from the mission field they are meant to serve right outside their doors. We find it intriguing, however, that while churches are dying and being closed at what seems to be alarming rates in mainline denominations, there are also signs of a great spiritual awakening in our culture unlike anything Kim and I have seen in more than thirty years of ministry together. Spiritual conversations seem to come more easily now and are encouraged even on popular prime-time talk shows like *Oprah*. Rock stars and movie stars have become the purveyors—postmodern evangelists, if you will—of a new kind of cultural religion that includes humanitarian and philanthropic enterprises. New forms of Christian faith communities are emerging in such nonconventional places as tattoo parlors, pubs, art studios, and coffee houses.

Pollsters like George Gallup and George Barna speak of this renewed interest in spiritual things but then painfully remind us of the continued decrease in the number of persons in the United States who consider themselves "churched." Can we assume that a vast number of these spiritually sensitive people are no longer turning to the organized church for guidance in their spiritual quest or to experience the Divine? Have mainline Protestant churches, which flourished in a Christendom culture and throughout the modern era, been too slow to respond to the rapid changes of the postmodern world around us? Are we as leaders in the church still operating under the assumption that when it comes to matters of religion and faith, the church is still the vendor of choice for people? That someday the world will wake up and return to us?

Kim and I recently met with the members of one of Hope-Spring's newest small groups. The average age of the participants is around thirty. Most are young families with elementary-school-aged children. I was asked by the leader to talk about my vision for the new church and especially the small groups we are starting throughout the area. I began by affirming their group and pointing out how we would love to multiply the experience they were having together. I emphasized how in this new church I believed pastoral care is not something everyone could automatically expect of me as the pastor. I talked about the ineffectiveness of that older model and how much more natural and helpful it would be for members of our small groups to learn to care for one another in times of crisis or concern. So instead of calling the pastor (me) whenever someone had a need, it made more sense for the members of their group to be notified and be mobilized into acts of care and compassion. No one in the group challenged my thoughts. In fact they looked at me as if to say, "Well, duh!" I think I was the only person in the room who thought about doing pastoral care the "old" way. They were already ahead of me.

Then came the question, "If the life of the church is in its smaller faith communities and we nurture and care for one another in the journey of faith, why do we need to be part of the larger church [referring to worship on Sunday morning] and give our money to support buildings, upkeep and maintenance, and a staff?" I saw where this was heading and confessed that I too have often wondered about these same things. I left that meeting encouraged by the honest conversations we had but found myself confused about my role as pastor of this new church. What *do* they need me for? Is there a better way to *be* the church and *do* ministry than I am even aware of? Can *I* imagine anything different than the picture of the church I have seen and supported all these years? The only answer I have come up with is this: What choice do I have but to imagine a different way? If we are to be faithful to God's call as leaders in the church we *have* to be willing to imagine how different things can and should be in the church.

Now Is the Time

After nearly thirty years of ministry together, Kim and I believe now is the time to creatively reimagine the church. As you will read in the following pages, we are not of the mindset of some that the church has become completely passé and irrelevant in our postmodern world. We acknowledge that we live in a different era from when the two of us started in ministry. And, like the generations of faithful people before us who were asked to imagine and interpret the things of God to a hungry and hurting world, we must learn to paint outside the lines, take some risks, stop being afraid of messing up the picture, and begin to experience for ourselves a new opportunity to work with the Divine. As Dr. Munson reminded us, "If we don't see it, they won't see it!" If we can't begin to imagine the Creative One transforming us and filling us with the magnificent colors of purpose and passion, how will we convey that to the culture around us?

An Imaginative Exercise for Groups

Divide your group into teams of four to six people. Give each team a sheet of newsprint and a box of crayons of thin colored markers. Explain the following exercise:

1. Draw a picture of your church one line at a time by one person at a time.
2. Make sure all team members are given a chance to add to the picture, one line at a time.
3. Absolutely no talking allowed.
4. You have twenty minutes to complete your picture.

After the time has expired, each team stands and shares their picture with the rest of the group. Each team should describe how the process worked for them—what went well and what went wrong, who became the leader of the group, why they portrayed their church as they did, and so on. Wrap up by pointing out the similarities and differences in the groups' portrayals of their church.

Reflection Questions

1. Name some of the major changes you have experienced in the world around you in your lifetime.
2. What was your first experience of the church?

3. How has your experience or understanding of the church changed in the last ten years?

4. What are some of the major changes your congregation has had to make in the way it does its ministry over the past decade? How well has your congregation adapted to this change?

5. What kind of changes will your congregation need to make in order to discover or continue effective ministry in a postmodern age?

CHAPTER 2

❧

Imagining a Visionary Church

*I*t amazes me how our actions as Christians really do affect other people. One Sunday as the praise band I sing in was leading the congregation, I noticed a neighbor come into the worship area and find a seat in the back. After I was finished on stage, I went and sat with him until I needed to go up front again. I simply made sure he was comfortable and was following along with our worship service. He was someone Gary and I had talked with about church and he had expressed interest in coming, so I really didn't think too much about what was happening. In the weeks that followed, his wife and son joined him, and they became regular attendees at worship and our home group. This particular group was made up of mostly neighbors we had invited to our church. We met every other week to get to know each other better and talk about our everyday experiences of living our faith. When he was able to tell our home group about their transition to the church, he broke down and wept about his take on my actions that morning. He was overwhelmed by them. He could not understand why I would show so much love and care towards him that I would come to sit with him. To me, I was simply noticing someone and showing a kindness. To him, my companionship was a pathway to salvation. We never know the impact simple actions have toward others.

Galatians 5:22–23, which lists the fruits of the Spirit, is one of my favorite scripture passages. It lays out for us, in a simple list, a framework for Christian behavior. I especially like the way Christian Schwartz, founder of the powerful Natural Church Development process for church health and growth, interprets this passage in his book *The Three Colors of Love*. He talks about the fact that there was no punctuation in the original Greek texts of the Bible. Instead of using only the commas we see in traditional translations, Schwartz suggests we add a colon, as in, "The fruit of the Spirit is love [as exemplified by]: joy, peace, patience, kindness, goodness, faithfulness, gentleness, and self-control." When we punctuate the verse this way, we see we have just one fruit—love, and the different ways in which we can live it.[1] For my neighbor, I was showing love through the kindness of noticing him and not wanting him to feel alone during our worship time. God used this simple act to transform a family and bring them closer to God. Wow.

Another scripture passage that is an important reminder to me of how we should live in Christian community comes from Jesus in Matthew 18. As Matthew lays out the chapter, we hear Jesus's response to the disciples who had asked about who will be greatest in the kingdom of heaven, Jesus's parable of the lost sheep, a teaching about a brother who sins against you, followed by Peter's question about forgiveness: How many times should I forgive? Jesus says, seventy times seven (v. 22 NLT). As the chapter progresses, we encounter teachings on humility, paying attention to the lost, and dealing with sin, followed by a very hard story about the perils of not forgiving or repenting.

When Peter asks the question about how many times we should forgive, he had no idea how Jesus would answer. The rabbis of Jesus's day taught that forgiving someone three times was enough. By asking if seven times was sufficient, Peter thought he was going way beyond what Jesus would require. But seventy times seven—now that is a lot of forgiving. I think Jesus was trying to tell us that forgiveness must be a primary practice of his followers, because by forgiving we are demonstrating God's love for each person. And yet, it is one of those things that we struggle with on a daily basis. We hold grudges, we fight within our congregations, and we find little things to hold over people so that we can get our own way. We don't live in community as Christians the way that Jesus wants us to. This hurts us as a church. Our reputation is tarnished because the community outside the walls sees how we treat one another and says, "What hypocrites!"

It Was Curtains for Me

Some of the most important relationships I have formed in my career as a preacher's wife developed when we lived in a suburb of Pittsburgh. Gary was the associate pastor of a large congregation, and for the first time we were living in an area where there were a lot of people our age. I began my life in this congregation much as I always did—I joined a Sunday school class. Unlike other congregations I had joined, this one actually had a class for young adults. What a thrill! As it turned out, several women my age also had advanced degrees in their chosen fields and were now staying at home raising children, all of them about the same ages as ours. This had never happened before. Within a few months, we had established a daytime playgroup and date nights with our husbands, and we were celebrating many holidays together. Not since high school had I developed such meaningful relationships.

Several months after I joined the Sunday school class, we decided to study the Myers-Briggs Type Indicator, since much had been written about how to apply this particular tool to a life of faith. We took the inventory and over a few weeks unpacked how our different personalities functioned in our marriages and our participation throughout the life of the church. I am an ISTJ. Now, this is a "brass corner" personality, which to my understanding means that this personality just doesn't change much and doesn't like to change. I once saw a T-shirt with a slogan that was a perfect fit for the ISTJ personality type: "Rules, Rituals, Regulations, and Always Right!" Yes, this is me. I claim it wholeheartedly. This personality is the person you come to when you want something done efficiently and correctly. We play by the rules, and we are very rarely wrong. We operate out of a sense of duty and do what "ought" to be done. I function best in a structured environment, especially where there are tasks to be done. In the years since I have taken this survey, I have once tested as an extrovert, but this just makes me more vocal about how right I am!

Not surprisingly, my Sunday school class, now also my social group, immediately took me up on who I was. They asked me to organize the date night co-op, and I eventually led the after-school program for the elementary school kids. We got things done efficiently and correctly—and they loved me for it!

Well, as life happens, things changed over the seven or eight years I participated in this group. (Remember—people with my personality type don't experience change well.) People moved, children started growing up, and our circle changed. Gary began a new ministry position with a capital fund-raising organization, and our family moved into a new house in Cranberry Township, still close enough to attend this particular church and worship together as a family. Since Gary was not serving a congregation and was traveling across the country throughout the week, my continued participation in this congregation was very important for our boys and me.

Not long after we moved, as we were still settling into our new home, I decided to make some valances for our front room windows. A task to do. I knew I had a day coming up when the boys would be at day camp, Gary would be working, and I would have a significant chunk of the day to do this task. Days like this just didn't happen for me very often, so I was locked into my task—sew those valances.

Unfortunately, one of those friends from that original class was going to be in town that day (they had moved away some months earlier). I am sure you can see where this is going—I chose to make my valances rather than go visit with my friend. Now I know this was the wrong choice. I knew that even as I made it, and the fallout was huge.

Several months later, I saw this friend when she came to town for a funeral. I was ready to apologize, to deal with the fact that I had made the wrong choice, and to make the amends necessary to get back on the right track with her and several others in the same group. So I walked up to her to begin this process, and she turned away. I still experience that awful wrenching feeling in the pit of my being like I did then, when I realized I had done something that she found unforgivable.

It took some time for me to process what had happened. There were several sleepless nights and lots of calling out to God before I finally realized that the unforgivable part was hers, not mine. I was who I was—task oriented, structured, working the plan, and finally willing to repent. I could have been forgiven by my friend, but she was hurt and unwilling at that time to forgive. I never saw her again.

It is now about ten years since this event happened. Obviously, because I am writing about it, this incident has become formational for me. Not being forgiven for choosing task over friend has helped me to keep my choices clearer. Since I now recognize that I tend to choose tasks over people, I think through those choices when they occur. Maybe that is why it was possible for me to even notice that our neighbor had come into worship and was sitting alone.

The Main Thing Is Love and Forgiveness

Love and forgiveness—they are the main objectives for how we live as a community of Christians. For a large part of my career, I have been a church consultant. I have worked as a workshop leader to train Sunday school teachers and with the leadership teams of many congregations to help them determine vision and set goals. I am now leading a networks of pastors and church leaders in personal spiritual renewal and church revitalization. I have been involved in nine congregations as a pastor's wife. Having been involved at different levels within the lives of many congregations, I can say that many would be more fruitful in their ministry if they practiced love and forgiveness—first among themselves and then in their communities. Love is the fruit of God's Spirit. It is exhibited ultimately in the action of Jesus dying on the cross for the salvation of each person. As followers of Jesus, we daily exhibit that love by practicing joy, peace, patience, kindness, goodness, faithfulness, gentleness, and self-control toward others.

Those who are truly repentant, who want to turn their lives around and walk yoked with Jesus, will also practice forgiveness. Remember the story with which Matthew 18 ends? The servant who owed much begged for forgiveness and was in fact forgiven by the king. But he showed he wasn't really repentant. His action toward the man who owed him money was deplorable and did not reflect the forgiveness he received. His forgiveness by the king was rescinded and he was thrown in prison until his debt was paid.

This difficult scripture passage shows us the value of a forgiving spirit and the harsh consequences of an unrepentant heart. Maybe the main thing—even more than love and forgiveness—is repentance. When we can be a community of people who are willing to put the needs of others first, then those outside the community of faith will be more readily drawn by who we are and what we do to the God who loves and forgives us all. Everyone wants to be loved, and everyone wants to be forgiven. This is the first part of being a visionary church.

As all good educators do, I keep my eyes open for materials that will illustrate important concepts I am teaching. Not long ago I came across an article in our local Sunday paper that I think illustrates the benefits of Christian behavior lived out in community and how those behaviors can attract others to the church. The writer, anthropology professor Robert L. Moore, had been studying Chinese society in Beijing and was surprised to meet a large number of recently converted Chinese Christians. He began to inquire about this phenomenon and discovered that many of the Chinese Christian churches, both Protestant and Catholic, are underground movements. One young woman described her former life as one of spiritual emptiness, especially given the now prevalent consumerism that drives Chinese society. This woman began to learn about Christianity through an American with whom she practiced English. Later, through the testimony of a Chinese Christian professor, she was led to an underground Protestant church. Her own testimony continues, "So you get good grades, so what? So you can buy things, so what? So you have a good husband and a child, so what? Christianity offers something more in life, something of value. The people in the church are like a family to each other. They are also a source of comfort." It seemed to me that this young Chinese woman was looking for a deeper place for living, a place that would require something from her. She did not want things and good relationships just for their own sakes or for what they would give her. She wanted something that went beyond her to envelop others around her. She wanted that "family" that could offer her comfort, love, and forgiveness and then in turn support her ability to offer love and forgiveness to others. What intrigued Moore was that this deeper place to live would attract people to it. What interests me is that this attraction has nothing to do with church buildings and programs. Rather, it is about people who are living authentically with each other, trying to find deeper meaning in their lives.[2]

Eric Van Meter, United Methodist campus minister at Arkansas State University, argues that the questions we ask determine the answers we get. Some of the typical questions being asked by church leaders include, "Where are our young adults? How do we attract people to this church we love?" Van Meter indicates that the answers elude us. My take is that we simply don't want to hear the answers, sometimes because they require us to do something we think is too hard and sometimes because they reflect poorly on us as faith communities and are therefore painful to hear. Van Meter, however, offers some new questions: "What does it mean to live in authentic Christian community? What characteristics do we as a community of faith want to embody? What is God up to in the world around us and how can we be a part of that?"[3] These are powerful questions, ones that will cause us to reflect on our life together as a congregation and that will also help us deal with the answers to the previous questions, such as, where are the young adults and how do we attract people to the church? Maybe if we learn to live authentically with God's help, others will be attracted to God as well.

Moore and Van Meter both make the case that the way Christians act, the basis for our reputation within our communities, is more important than the programs churches offer, especially when it comes to attracting new and younger people to the established church. Again, this comes back to love, repentance, and forgiveness within the body of Christ. When my neighbor came to our church for the first time, it really didn't matter to him that we worshiped in an elementary school or that the furnishings were stored in the trailer that was parked in our driveway throughout the week. What mattered to him was whether the people in this place would extend kindness, friendship, and genuine love for him and his family. The reason he stayed and brought his wife and son had everything to do with his perception of how he could fit in and whether he felt he could connect to God through this church gathering. His questions were, will this group of people make room for me? Are they really who they appear to be?

A Recipe for Disaster

For a family such as ours, who has been doing the "Sunday routine" for many years, one of the really fun things about planting new churches is that there are sometimes periods when there is more flexibility in that routine. We experienced this during the first part of 2007 when the new congregation Gary was appointed to plant was in its practice phase, meeting only once a month.[4] Another pastor in the area asked Gary to fill her pulpit while she was on vacation, and since it was Communion Sunday, she needed an ordained pastor to serve the communion elements. Gary accepted the opportunity, and we went to this church to experience a bit of what other folks see when they go church shopping.

When we arrived at the church, we were greeted warmly, shown around, and allowed to acclimate to the surroundings, which was especially important for Gary as the guest preacher. As the service was about to begin, I found a place in the congregation, Gary found his place on the platform, and worship began. The choir was wonderful and the congregation enthusiastic—until the announcement time.

Evidently this was the day when the women's group was first offering its new cookbook. The dear lady who got up to make the announcement was very dignified but obviously shaken about something. As she proceeded to tell us about the cookbooks and what the proceeds were going to support—it finally came out. In the final process of editing the cookbook before it went to the printer—one recipe had been omitted. Now from my seat, from which I was able to see the woman making the announcement, I could also see the woman whose recipe had been omitted. It was obvious to me—a total stranger in this congregation—that the one whose recipe was accidentally omitted was the worst person to whom this could have happened.

The announcement lady kept looking over at the offended woman, quietly offering apologies, desperately wanting to be publicly forgiven. Nothing. The offended one sat staring straight ahead, not acknowledging the announcement or the offered apology. It was unbelievable. This went on for quite a few minutes, until the announcement lady finally took her seat and the worship service moved ahead. Luckily Gary was really "on" that day, and the service picked up its momentum and ended well.

After the service we bumped into the offended one on our way out of the sanctuary. It was obvious to me that she intended to be offended until the second coming of Jesus. Part of me chuckled all the way home because I knew this experience would be one that I could use in my teaching! I can't tell you how many church cookbooks I have. As a preacher's wife and a sometimes guest speaker at women's group meetings, I have seen them all. Nearly every cookbook has a recipe pasted on the inside back cover to correct an error, so I know errors are not difficult to fix. But another part of me wondered what if someone new to that community had been in worship that day and had seen what I saw? Time and again we demonstrate that we still haven't figured out how to live a discipled Christian life well enough to do it on a regular basis. How can we attract people to the church and connect them to God when it is so obvious that we aren't practicing what we preach?

Today we hear awful stories about the behavior of the clergy. We hear of extramarital affairs, abuses within clergy families, and sexual abuse of children by clergy, and we should hear about those things. They point out to us that we are all flawed human beings—constantly in need of love and repentance and forgiveness and rehabilitation. Clergy hold a place in society from which a fall from grace is nearly unforgivable. In the past ten years the media has inundated us with stories about fallen clergy, so we are beginning to be thicker-skinned about it. But we need to hear about these sins, because all of us, not only clergy, need to be held accountable for living up to Jesus's example.

All church participants are called by the ancient rites of baptism, confirmation, and membership to practice the same standards of behavior within their community. I am talking about love: joy, peace, patience, kindness, goodness, gentleness, faithfulness, and self-control. Other behaviors—like obedience, repentance, forgiveness, and humility—are important too. These behaviors show a depth of intimacy with our risen Savior. When a person like Eric Van Meter asks what it means to live in authentic Christian community, we should be able to point to such a community, one where loving one another is more important that judging one another. When a stranger comes into our midst, we should be able to offer a place at the family table so that they can feast and grow strong in their own relationship with Jesus. When a catastrophe happens in the community, imagine members of the church rising to their feet and standing by the side of those in need with justice and mercy. When one in our own body of Christ sins, we should be able to offer forgiveness and guidance on a path toward wholeness.

Pastor and scholar Eugene Peterson offers this translation of a passage from Jesus's Sermon on the Mount: "Don't look for shortcuts to God. The market is flooded with surefire, easygoing formulas for a successful life that can be practiced in your spare time. Don't fall for that stuff, even though crowds of people do. The way to life—to God!—is vigorous and requires total attention" (Matt. 7:13–14, *The Message*).

I would never say that living the Christian life was easy; sometimes it is downright difficult. Other translations of this same passage in Matthew talk about entering through the narrow gate. There is a wide gate you can enter and a broad road you can travel, but it is often paved with destruction. I often have to drive on a broad road on my way to the office on the other side of Orlando. I get a sense that if each driver were vigorously paying attention to the road and what was happening on it, fewer accidents and less destruction would occur than what I regularly see. My overwhelming sense is that very few people actually care about what is going on outside their own vehicle. They only want to get to where they are going as fast as possible with little or no regard for those around them. Sometimes I am one of them when I am behind the wheel—Gary would tell you I am *all* of them! But we need to remember the narrow gate—like a toll booth, not the ones you can zoom through at sixty-five miles per hour but the ones that have a narrow entrance and a bar that goes up and down once you pay your money. We need to pay attention and be diligent to get through those gates. If we want our churches to be places where people can connect with God and grow to become the kind of people that God wants them to be, then every person within the body needs to practice love: joy, peace, patience, kindness, goodness, gentleness, faithfulness, and self-control.

Picture This

The goal that every Christian would reflect the biblical mandate to do justice, love mercy, and walk humbly with God (Mic. 6:8) sounds darn near impossible to reach. But if we want the church, our church, to become a place that attracts the folks who are seeking a deeper relationship with God, then this is the direction we must be aiming. We can imagine a church where folks are striving to create a community that fully reflects God's love, but how do we do that?

A powerful picture, a vision, of that community must be painted for each local church to motivate each individual within the church toward this end. Vision is motivating, captivating, vibrant, and, with some work, reachable. A vision helps us imagine a more God-centered future. Bill Hybels, senior pastor of Willow Creek Community Church in the Greater Chicago area, in his opening remarks at the 2007 Leadership Summit, defined vision as "a powerful picture that produces passion in people."[5]

When I first started in the "vision business"—leading workshops and working with leadership teams to develop vision for their congregations, we worked mainly toward a vision of what the church wanted to do. All well and good—everyone knows that the things we *do* are achievable—we can measure and count them, decide when they are done and whether they were worthwhile. But in many instances, such visions simply promoted the kind of inward thinking already pervasive within churches.

I mentioned earlier the large suburban church in the Pittsburgh area that Gary served as an associate pastor. Part of his job in this particular church was to help leaders and members redefine their vision for the congregation. He worked for a year with a group of dedicated leaders through a specific process to make sure that the vision would inspire an imaginative picture to move them into the future. This particular congregation already had excellent ministries for children and youth, so the vision that emerged was one that would concentrate this congregation's efforts toward the children and youth in the community, creating places where children, youth, and their families would experience God's love. The newly defined vision had the potential to move this church into a preferred future.

Now as often happens when a congregation commits to a new sense of direction and purpose, there were grumblings. Mostly the grumblings came from the older folks who wanted to know how this new vision would serve them. The leaders of the visioning process encouraged them to think of a new future where they could be mentors for children and youth, a place where their grandchildren could grow to love Jesus. They were encouraged to get involved by volunteering for Sunday school or preschool programs. And for the most part, they were happy to begin working toward this new future.

Then, more changes came about. Gary took the job with the capital stewardship company, the senior pastor retired, and a new pastor was appointed. After a few months, this new pastor went off on a spiritual retreat and came back with a new vision for this congregation. I am not really sure why it was necessary to discern a new vision, especially because this pastor was coming with a stated interest in children and youth, or why this pastor felt it was his job alone to develop this vision, but that is what happened. When he came back from his retreat and shared his vision with the leadership, it was readily accepted. The new vision included a statement about sharing the spark of God's light and love with "people like us." When this was shared from the pulpit, I could feel my heart sink into my stomach. It was a safe vision, especially for introverted people who often struggle with reaching out to folks. It was a sanitized vision, without a bit of the messiness that often comes with change and new direction. And it was a simple vision, because it meant that we really didn't need to change the way we were doing things in order to accomplish it.

Over the next ten years, this vision led this congregation to a difficult place. The worship attendance gradually dropped, the interest in children and youth dwindled, and while there were always vital ministries within this church, they were mostly inward focused. Today I checked out the congregation's website because

I knew that a change in senior pastor leadership had occurred about a year ago. Now their vision is, "Reaching people with the good news of Jesus Christ, and together, becoming fully devoted followers of Christ." This vision is less safe, is a little more difficult, and might get a little messy. Because the first word is "reaching," I am assuming that this church is learning something about getting beyond themselves and their own needs in order to make a difference in the community around them.

I like an illustration from Joel Barker's video, *The Power of Vision*.[6] Barker was the first person to popularize the idea of paradigm shifts for the corporate world, making room for new thinking in the midst of the way things have always been done. In this video, he asks viewers to imagine a rope thrown across a rushing waterway and tied to the other side. This is a vision tied to a preferable future. The rope helps us cross the rushing water in the same way that holding on to a newly imagined future helps us through the daily strains of life. This is a marvelous way for the church to think of vision, but it demands from us that we first imagine a picture of that future. What I have learned in this "vision business" is that visioning a different future for our church (inward focused) is not the whole picture. We must begin visioning a new future for our community (outward focused) because our church exists within that community. When we can picture our community as a God-filled place, then we have created a powerful picture that produces passion in people.

The Scripture teaches us very clearly about imagined pictures of a new future. In the book of Isaiah, the prophet sees a new vision for the people. Isaiah 29 states: "In a very short time, will not Lebanon be turned into a fertile field and the fertile field seem like a forest? In that day the deaf will hear the words of the scroll, and out of gloom and darkness the eyes of the blind will see. Once more the humble will rejoice in the LORD; the needy will rejoice in the Holy One of Israel" (vv. 17–19 NIV).

Fast forward to Luke 7: "At that very time Jesus cured many who had diseases, sicknesses and evil spirits, and gave sight to many who were blind. So he replied to the messengers, 'Go back and report to John what you have seen and heard: The blind receive sight, the lame walk, those who have leprosy are cured, the deaf hear, the dead are raised, and the good news is preached to the poor. Blessed is the man who does not fall away on account of me'" (vv. 21–23 NIV). The proof of Isaiah's imagined vision of a new future was realized in the actions of Jesus. Jesus knew that John the Baptist would recognize the reality of that vision fulfilled, thus answering the questions in John's mind about the truth of Jesus.

For our purposes, Isaiah's vision captures something else. The work of the Lord was in what happened outside the walls of the temple and synagogues. The blind were seeing, the deaf were hearing. It wasn't that the people of faith were growing deeper in their understanding of the Scriptures or that there were more opportunities for the people of faith to participate in classes or programs. The imagined vision affected the community outside the walls. The unclean, impure, and untouchable were being changed! No wonder this evidence of God produced passion in people.

Vision Starts with the Heart

The churches I am working with right now in a "reFocusing" process will eventually be called to revision for themselves.[7] They will first be given the opportunity to look back at their history—to name it and claim it—and if necessary experience repentance and forgiveness in order to move forward. Looking back allows the congregation to imagine, based on the successes of the past, who God made them to be. Next they will begin to recognize the wider community by studying the demographics of their zip code area. They will name and claim their own demographic makeup within the congregation and begin the work of ministering beyond themselves to the rest of their community. When they have a realistic picture of who they are (past and present), they can begin to imagine who God made them to be through a series of prayer opportunities, focus groups, and worship emphases. Out of this process they will develop a clearer picture of a work they can do with God in their community. The process of new vision is trying to get in line with what God is already doing. For some of these congregations, a new vision may mean building bridges toward the immigrant populations in their communities, it may mean recognizing the pockets of poverty that exist right under their noses, or it may mean reaching out to the children and youth who walk by the church on their way to and from school. The final step for these churches in the reFocusing process is to evaluate what they do now as it relates to this new vision—probably changing some things that just don't fit anymore in order to make room for God's new direction. This is the strategy work of vision—determining how we move across that rush of water to where God is calling us to be. If a vision is just a nice thing on a piece of paper, it is worthless. A vision must move us forward into the future by holding us accountable, like that rope across the rushing water, day by day and year by year, until we reach a point where our picture is nearly complete and we need to find a new picture to pull us into new futures that are yet unimagined.

I started this chapter by talking about our personal behavior as Christians within our congregations. We practice love, forgiveness, and repentance within the church so that when the opportunity for making an impact on our community comes, we are ready for those who may arrive in the congregation as a result of that vision. I am reminded of an older member of one of our churches who stood in the back of the sanctuary appearing to welcome folks to worship. However, she was overheard telling the younger people, "If all you new folks keep coming here, there won't be any room for us older folks." I am sure some people were turned away by her comments. Each person's behavior affects the congregation's ability to hold on to that rope and actually make the journey toward the powerful picture of God's vision within our community.

Some years ago, a local politician in Orange County, Florida, got caught with a prostitute. Although he lost almost everything dear to him, his story is one of confession, repentance (turning

around), and the forgiveness given by his wife and the congregation he belongs to. The politician immediately came clean when
faced with his indiscretion: "I didn't want to go the route of being
a victim. We're all sinners, we all sin. It's what you do with it that
matters." His pastor later claimed: "There was a season of earning
that trust back. But it would have been completely hypocritical
for us to turn our back on him when we know what we've been
forgiven of. And he was repentant. He didn't make excuses."[8]

Do you think this man belongs to a congregation that attracts
other folks? You bet. According to their website, they are actively
involved in planting other congregations around the world. Many
of the leaders in the existing church see themselves as missionaries to the new congregations. They spread love and forgiveness
wherever they go.

In 2006 the Amish community in Nickel Mines, Pennsylvania,
was devastated when a gunman killed six children at their school.
In the days that followed this tragedy, the Amish community found
ways to begin forgiving the gunman, who was also killed. One way
they acted on this was by attending the killer's funeral. More than
half the people who attended that funeral were Amish wanting to
reach out to his family. Steven M. Nolt, coauthor of *Amish Grace:
How Forgiveness Transcended Tragedy*, learned through his inves-
tigation of this Amish community how pervasive forgiveness is
in the theology and practice of the Amish tradition. Nolt writes:
"Their understanding of forgiveness is that it is a long process,
that it is difficult, that it is painful, that replacing bitter feelings
toward someone is something that takes time, and they would
say that happens only through God's grace. But they begin with
expressing their intention to forgive, with the faith that the emotional forgiveness will follow over months and years. They don't
begin with trying to blame someone or something."[9]

Granted, the Amish community does not attract a lot of converts, but this event stands as an unequaled example of forgiveness extended toward the outside world. The foundational beliefs
of the Amish community are rooted in their deep and abiding
faith in their own forgiveness by a loving God. Their collective

vision, whether they express it or not, is to extend that grace and forgiveness to others. We can be touched by their example, even if we can't live their lifestyle.

Imagining a Visionary Church

When we look back over the ideas expressed in this chapter, it becomes obvious that reputation and integrity are essential to who the church is and what the church does. Ultimately we want people outside the church walls to view those who are within in a good light, so that those outside can also experience God's love for them in an overwhelming way. We want to be known as people who care, people who want a better life for everyone, people who can be counted on to help when times get tough, people who will share God's love for humanity in as obvious a way as possible. That is about reputation.

But we also want to be experienced as people who walk and talk the same language, and that is about integrity. To do this we have to be clear about God's vision for our local congregation. We need to have a picture in our minds about where God is already working in our community with us as partners. We have to be inspired by God's picture of a different and preferable future, because it is God who is leading and directing us to that end. And we have to lift up Christian character and behavior, as exhibited by Jesus, as a norm for our lives together within the walls of the church and when we rub elbows with the world. Remember, Christian character is living with love as our operative, exhibited by joy, peace, patience, kindness, goodness, faithfulness, gentleness, and self-control. We must keep repentance and forgiveness as our primary behaviors toward each other.

When I realize how difficult it is to actually do what I just wrote, I immediately think of Romans 12:2 in the New Living Translation: "Don't copy the behavior and customs of this world, but let God transform you into a new person by changing the way you think. Then you will learn to know God's will for you, which is good and pleasing and perfect." We take great heart in knowing that it is God who transforms us, God who stands with us, and God who ultimately gave us God's Son, Jesus, so that we could be reconciled with God. This is such good news we can't help but share it with the world.

Reflection Questions

Now it is time for a hard look at how the ideas expressed in this chapter are played out in your congregation. Gather some spiritually mature folks and work through these questions together.

1. In what areas within the life of your congregation do you need to do the hard work of repentance and forgiveness?
2. How does your congregation exhibit the fruits of love listed in Galatians: joy, peace, patience, kindness, goodness, faithfulness, gentleness, and self-control?
3. Prayerfully consider how your congregation can begin to take steps to rectify areas where the fruits of love are not exhibited.
4. Look at your church's vision statement. Does it reflect the community outside the walls of the church building? What might be a first step in identifying a community need that your church can meet?
5. What resources does your congregation need in order to be an example of Christian behavior and character within your community?

❦

CHAPTER 3

Imagining a Transforming Congregation

*M*y home church, Evangelical United Brethren Church, was the big downtown church in the little town of Hummelstown, nestled between Harrisburg and Hershey in the rolling hills of central Pennsylvania. The church, built with huge gray stones, stood on the corner of Main and Hanover Streets. The Shultz family began attending worship there when I was around five years old and became a member of the Brownie troop the congregation sponsored. In my mind's eye I can still see our little group of Brownies—dressed in our Brownie dresses with Brownie beanies that looked surprisingly like Hershey's Kisses. This probably explains my lifelong love affair with chocolate!

One of my most significant memories happened when I was ten. The sanctuary was long and narrow with a pulpit and lectern that loomed above us. Every week at the eleven o'clock service just after the Sunday school hour, our family filed into what we thought of as "our pew"—on the lectern side, about six rows back.

On this special day in 1968, the congregation was voting on a new name because our denomination, the Evangelical United Brethren Church, had merged with The Methodist Church to become The United Methodist Church. At that time this meant very little to me, except for the opportunity to decide on a new name for our congregation. I remember two choices: Trinity United Methodist Church or Evangelical United Methodist Church. I voted for Evangelical because it was a name I already knew, and I enjoyed the way it rolled off my tongue. More people voted for Trinity, though, and so we became. Losing the vote was not what was important; being asked to vote was. For me, this simple act of checking off a name and placing my ballot in a shiny gold offering plate was significant, because now I had a place where I belonged, a place where my thoughts counted for something, even if the congregation as a whole chose the other name.

Those next ten years at Trinity United Methodist Church gave me a solid foundation in my Christian faith. I moved from the children's choir to the youth choir, and my parents enjoyed the move to the eight o'clock service when the youth choir sang.

I became a leader in the youth group, helping to plan retreats and outings, where we flirted with each other and played "Honey If You Love Me, Won't You Please Just Smile." Those years in the youth group were so significant to my Christian walk. We experienced not only the regular programs of youth groups but also the love of great youth leaders. Two young couples opened their homes and lives to us as teenagers. They provided listening ears, open arms, a willingness to learn Scripture with us, and the chance to grow.

The summer after my junior year at West Virginia Wesleyan College, I returned to my beloved Trinity UMC, where they hired me as a summer intern. I was able to plan worship, visit shut-ins with the pastors, and help lead the liturgy on Sunday mornings. Gary and I were already dating, so we had a good time sharing worship resources and experiences, his from serving a dying inner city congregation, and mine from working at the large downtown congregation.

All of these memories provide a framework for me to talk about the work of making disciples. As a child, a youth, then a young woman, this church provided the early experiences of teaching and learning, practicing and participating that made me the Christian I am today. For that, I am so grateful, and I will always remember the names and faces of those who helped inform, form, and transform me.

Three Graced Movements

John Wesley, the founder of the Methodist movement in the 1700s, had a great idea about transformation. For Wesley, the Christian life was like a journey on which each individual experiences God's grace, or unmerited favor, in three ways. First, we receive "prevenient" grace—one of the great words of the Methodist faith. Prevenient grace is the action of God in an individual life, which comes before the person is aware of it and causes a person to connect in a meaningful way with God. For me, prevenient grace was the action of God that placed me in the loving arms of Christian parents who not only encouraged me to go to church and Sunday school, but also went to their own classes and attended worship faithfully. For some, this action of God involves the interaction of a mysterious set of circumstances that eventually leads a person to faith. I have heard many testimonies from people who have had dramatic conversion experiences—living on their own, far away from God—and yet being able to respond to God because of a friend's witness or a song or a near-death experience. Wesley believed that the movement of God leading folks to find him, even in their sinfulness, was God's prevenient grace. It is God's action that propels a person toward God.

The second movement of faith Wesley called justification, or "justifying grace." This type of grace is typically thought of as the time when individuals reach a point in their own lives where they are finally willing to give God control and become a follower of Jesus. This grace is a free gift of God, given for all, but it is each person's free will to choose it or not. Justification is that moment when I become, in God's eyes, *just-as-if-I'd* never sinned. In a sermon he preached at Bristol in 1740, Wesley states:

> The grace or love of God, whence cometh our salvation, is *free in all*, and *free for all*. . . . It is free in all to whom it is given. It

does not depend on any power or merit in man; no, not in any degree, neither in whole, nor in part. It does not in anywise depend either on the good works or righteousness of the receiver; not on anything he has done, or anything he is. It does not depend on his endeavors. It does not depend on his good tempers, or good desires, or good purposes and intentions; for all these flow from the free grace of God; they are the streams only, not the fountain. They are the fruits of free grace, and not the root. They are not the cause, but the effects of it.[1]

I can remember first having the opportunity to make that decision for myself at a youth retreat when I was in seventh grade. About forty teens, most of them older than I, were seated in a circle around a desk in the center of the room. Our pastor invited us, as we wanted to, to go to the desk and pray to receive Jesus as our Savior. Well, no one went to that desk—but I prayed that prayer right where I sat, and I think it worked just as well. In the years since that retreat, I have prayed that prayer again plenty of times, and each time I have made a more meaningful commitment to being the person that God wants me to be by simply claiming that I am God's and God is mine.

This leads us to the third movement of faith called sanctification. "Sanctifying grace" was Wesley's term for what we might call "transformation." It is a lifelong process of change that takes us from being sinful people now willing to commit to Jesus to mature disciples who know that the true job of the disciple is to make more disciples. Sanctification involves prayer, Bible study, and discernment; exercising our spiritual gifts; and cultivating an obedient heart that makes us willing to follow God's lead throughout every day. For most Christians, sanctification is a process that they don't even realize is happening until one day, in some sort of circumstance, they realize they are different people than who they were before. Often we realize only in hindsight that we have been transformed.

This past year has been a transforming time for me. Our oldest son, soon to be nineteen, is now a college freshman. If someone had told me a year and a half ago that a child's eighteenth birthday provided an opportunity for that child to pass from childhood to adulthood in one fell swoop, I would have thought they were nuts. But for this child and our family that birthday was *huge*. Suddenly Aaron realized that we didn't have quite the same hold on him that we once had. As a legal adult, he now had some power. He decided that what we thought about his behavior just didn't matter that much to him. Now, he didn't start smoking, doing drugs, or doing other "bad" stuff—parents' nightmares—but he did start hanging out with friends, staying out late, and not telling us everything he was doing. My reaction to this change was one of total disbelief. I couldn't believe that all those years we invested in this young life were suddenly tossed aside for a life of his choosing. So I did what every self-respecting, loving mother would do—I began worrying. I couldn't sleep until I knew he was home; I began prowling around the house at night, making up scenarios in my head that were beyond nightmares; I became the crazy mom. All the while, Gary slept peacefully, completely oblivious to the hell I was imagining for myself.

Needless to say, this kind of behavior takes a toll on a person. I was loosing perspective and overreacting to nearly everything. The summer of 2007 will go down as my most stressful summer. But in the midst of that, a "still small voice" kept saying, "It will be OK." Some great friends had also lived through this and were able to encourage me by sharing their own stories of parenting. Despite the fact that Gary's sleeping and obliviousness to my situation was annoying, his calm did get through to me. Gary was able to put Aaron in God's hands before he went to bed, a feat that I had not been able to do. Actually I did through prayer put Aaron in God's hands—over and over and over again. But each night before I fell asleep, I took him back from God.

Transformation for me finally occurred when I realized that Aaron was coming home sober, that he was making his own kind of transformation from child to man, and that I needed to let him do that. I realize that the kind of mom I am for Aaron now is different from when he was little. I can support him without quashing him and love him without overwhelming him. When I was able to trust God's work in Aaron's life, then I could relax and help him get on with his growing up. I am not saying this was easy, or that it is over, but we are all working on trusting, loving, and praying together. I am working harder at being patient with Aaron: not standing in the way of him working out his own choices or jumping to conclusions for him or putting up roadblocks to his own learning though mistakes. In looking back, I can see God's grace—sanctifying this process through God's love for me. God's promise, "I will be with you," has had great sustaining power for me in the crazy-mom phase. In many ways I have learned throughout this experience to rely on God rather than on my own parenting skills.

Now, I share all this information with you about my denominational system of transformation for one important point. Unless each congregation is willing to grapple with the impact of transformation on individual lives and find ways to encourage it, facilitate it, and celebrate it, they are little more than organizations where patting each other on the back for individual accomplishments and encouraging the status quo are the norm.

Intentional Disciple Making for Transformation

Today we often use words like disciple making, transformation, and fully devoted followers to describe the results of sanctification within a congregation. Every one of the local churches I know has some type of class or small group that is meant to help believers become disciples. I think there are four important practices that help us move folks from believers to disciples: evangelize, establish, equip, and entrust. If every congregation intentionally built its disciple-making system on these four practices, I imagine congregations could really be transforming communities by encouraging relationships that move folks to deeper experiences of the Christian faith. I originally found these four action words in a book called *Disciplemaking: Training Leaders to Make Disciples.*[2] They were originally put together in a cyclical arrangement to show the movement from unbeliever to discipler. The idea has been expressed in many other resources, with lots of different words, but the point is that the work of making disciples is ongoing for congregations, and this happens when two things are occurring simultaneously.

First, *making* disciples is the foundational work of the congregation. Matthew 28:16–20 gives us the Great Commission—Jesus's words to inspire his church:

> Then the eleven disciples went to Galilee, to the mountain where Jesus had told them to go. When they saw him, they worshiped him; but some doubted. Then Jesus came to them and said, "All authority in heaven and on earth has been given to me. Therefore go and *make disciples* of all nations, baptizing them in the name of the Father and of the Son and of the Holy Spirit, and teaching them to obey everything I have commanded you. And surely I am with you always, to the very end of the age" (NIV, emphasis added).

Making disciples is a directive from Jesus; it is the purpose of the church.

Second, each individual Christian is to be a disciple, or *become* a disciple, by living a Christian life. How this happens is somewhat mysterious, yet faithful disciples are the evidence of a faithful congregation. Now I don't want to discredit those folks who are able to manage their growth as Christians on their own, but I have found that we can become disciples most effectively when we participate in Christian community. A congregation that supports individuals' growth in discipleship by both encouraging them and holding them accountable usually has a fruitful ministry overall.

EVANGELISM: SOWING SEEDS

The first part of this transformational process is to *evangelize.*
I realize that this can be a scary word. We immediately think of
preaching on a street corner or handing out tracts at the mall or
confronting every person we meet with the question, "Where are
you going if you die tonight?" I am not talking about that kind of
evangelism. I am talking about providing opportunities for people
to find Christ and respond to God's justifying grace. Then we are
partnering with God to create in individuals a desire to develop a
relationship with the God who loves them unconditionally.

I discovered an article in *USA Today* about the U.S. Religious
Landscape Survey conducted by the Pew Forum on Religion and
Public Life, which reported the fluidity of faith in American culture.[3] Forty-four percent of the folks interviewed state that they
are no longer tied to the religious or secular upbringing they experienced as children. They have changed religions or denominations, adopted a faith for the first time, or abandoned any relationship with a religion. While 51.3 percent of the folks interviewed
called themselves Protestant, about one-third of this group were
"unable or unwilling" to describe the denomination to which they
belonged. I have to wonder whether this reported lack of commitment to a religious group has anything to do with the individual's
commitment to the God those groups profess.

We can go through our whole lives in some congregations without ever being invited to respond to God's call on our lives. Do
you want to be a Christian? Do you want to be Jesus's friend? Do
you want to give your life to Jesus and become all that God wants
you to be? These evangelism questions are often not asked. How
can folks respond if they are not asked to acknowledge that God
has been doing something in their life (prevenient grace) and now
they can respond (justifying grace)? How can we make disciples if
we haven't asked folks to become followers? The responsibility of
every Sunday school teacher, small group leader, youth worker includes learning to be comfortable asking the questions that move
people toward faith, then knowing how to encourage the small

steps of faith into a pathway of sanctification. The decision to become a follower of Christ is itself enough for eternal life, but belief alone isn't enough to live in the fullness of all that God offers.

The church's work of evangelism has two parts. First, the church provides opportunities for folks to respond to God's love in a way that moves them toward making a decision to follow Jesus Christ as their personal Savior. Second, the church helps them move into the world to share the good news. Many congregations today are happily living within their facility's walls, working at affecting those few who come through the doors, encouraging discipleship among the faithful attendees. Evangelism is also the work of sharing the good news with the wider community. Today my husband got up early to take our minivan, loaded with water bottles, hand towels, and animal crackers, to Winter Garden for the Christmas Fun Run—a 5K race through downtown. He has the HopeSpring banner, the outdoor kiosk, and six or eight helpers to hand out the goodies. This is one way our congregation practices servant evangelism—meeting needs. The runners will be thirsty and sweaty, their children will be hungry, and our new church needs to build a positive reputation in its community. So we pull all those things together to provide an opportunity for God to work prevenient grace throughout the crowd.

Last week Gary went with some helpers to Winter Garden's Light-Up Night, a celebration when the community holiday decorations are lighted, and handed out candy to the children and talked with their parents about our congregation. One result of those conversations was a new family at worship the next Sunday morning, where they were introduced to our community of faith as we worshiped God together. God's work was begun! Next week we will be wrapping packages for Christmas shoppers at the new mall in the community. We provide the paper, bows, nametags, and wrappers. The shoppers are so glad to have this service provided free that they will take the little cards inviting them to HopeSpring's Christmas Eve services.

Evangelism is about providing opportunities for folks to discover and follow their own pathways to God through Jesus Christ, inside and outside the doors of the church building. Our congregations may not always see the end results of our efforts to evangelize. Sometimes we are planting seeds in people's lives that may not come to fruit until many more seeds have been planted. Jesus illustrates the idea of planting seeds in this familiar passage from the Gospel of Mark:

> [Jesus said,] "Listen! A farmer went out to sow his seed. As he was scattering the seed, some fell along the path, and the birds came and ate it up. Some fell on rocky places, where it did not have much soil. It sprang up quickly, because the soil was shallow. But when the sun came up, the plants were scorched, and they withered because they had no root. Other seed fell among thorns, which grew up and choked the plants, so that they did not bear grain. Still other seed fell on good soil. It came up, grew and produced a crop, multiplying thirty, sixty, or even a hundred times." Then Jesus said, "He who has ears to hear, let him hear" (4:3–9 NIV).

God's job is to nurture that seed and make it grow, ideally with the willing participation of the seed receiver, and the church's job is to faithfully sow as many seeds of God's grace as possible.

ESTABLISHING FAITH: FERTILIZING SEEDS

The second expression in this cycle of disciple making is *establish*. Trinity United Methodist Church established me in the faith as I attended Sunday school and participated in children's choir and youth activities. I already knew the Bible stories and many other stories of faith by the time I committed my life to Jesus Christ because I spent nearly every Sunday of my childhood with people who believed them and taught them. Sometimes this disciple-making process begins later because teens or adults who come to faith may not have had the Sunday school background that establishes faithful knowledge. So offering small groups or classes that start with beginning steps and move people forward to more advanced knowledge is very important. We have found that short-term introductory classes help people form basic ideas about the Bible, Jesus, and faithful living, especially if they are given some instruction on tools they can use in their own lives to continue learning, such as devotionals, different types of prayer, a Bible dictionary, or their own study Bibles. Advanced knowledge becomes very important for people who need a solid foundation when they begin to talk to their friends and neighbors about their faith journey. Nearly everyone wants to feel some degree of confidence about his or her faith story, so a more involved course, like *Disciple Bible Study* published by the United Methodist Publishing House, helps to solidify a person's understanding of the Scriptures.

I often think of the establishing step as answering the question, What do I need to know and understand in my head in order to move forward with my faith? If establishing is only pouring information into people's heads, then, especially for adults, their continued growth in Christian living is at risk, meaning they might want to participate in Bible study after Bible study without ever interacting in their community to share God's love. I have witnessed too many church school classes and small groups that have moved from study to study, year after year, and rarely moving beyond the classroom to actually live their Christian life in the real world. Pairing learning with doing helps folks retain and grow in their faith. When a class that studies what the Bible says about caring for the poor also makes a trip to the local food pantry and helps hand out food, then people experience something memorable that will hopefully produce Christians who are willing to take action. Providing ways to practice what participants are learning is essential in every class or small group, especially for youth and adults. Mission work, service projects, keeping prayer journals, sharing family devotions, and hundreds of other things can help us practice our faith while we learn.

The class environment must be a safe place for every person to experiment with his or her faith and to share those experiences with others by being open to what folks are experiencing throughout their week. When I am training teachers in the church, I often encourage them to begin their classes by briefly highlighting what the lesson was from the last time the class met. Before moving into new material, the teacher asks how that previous learning affected the students' week. The teachers may need to ask these questions several times before students are willing to share something, but eventually they will. Then at the end of the class, the teacher and students talk about what the current week's lesson has to do with living Christian lives throughout the week. The class identifies something they can practice because of their time together. For example, a lesson on prayer would lead participants to want to pray. The class might agree to try a specific type of prayer during the week. When the class comes back together, participants can report on what they experienced because of this assignment and identify ways that they are transforming their behavior because of these efforts. In 1969 Edgar Dale wrote a book called *Audio-Visual Methods in Teaching* in which he presented the "Cone of Learning." This cone tells us that particular teaching methods determine what and how much learners retain. When we only read something from printed material, we retain about 10 percent, when we see something like a picture or a video, we retain about 30 percent. Dale's cone helped educators understand that the cumulative effect of hearing, seeing, and doing something has the ability to help learners retain about 90 percent of the teaching.[4] Teachers and leaders can encourage students to practice faithful living through trial and error in order to produce disciples.

A good friend of mine is a great example of how faith can be established. He came to the church as a young dad, recently divorced, with an elementary-school-aged son. Bob had very little church background but had experienced some of those prevenient grace movements of God and found his way to a congregation. He and his son attended worship each week. One Sunday the pastor was asking for volunteers to teach Sunday school, and Bob responded. No one asked him specifically to teach Sunday school—he heard the request and responded to it. He spent the next five or six years teaching the four-year-olds and then worshiping with his son. Bob is now the chairperson of this congregation's leadership council, active in hunger ministry, and helping to launch our new congregation HopeSpring. He is one of the most dedicated Christian laymen I have known. I asked Bob once what helped him to become the mature Christian he is, especially since he didn't grow up in the church. His answer astounded me: "Teaching the four year olds"! Bob took an opportunity to establish his faith. By teaching these children, he learned the stories of faith, and so he was able to see God's activity throughout the Bible and find his own way to God through Jesus. He was able to learn the head knowledge he felt he needed at that time, and he became instrumental in helping the children become established in their faith. Talk about win-wins!

EQUIPPING FAITH: TENDING THE PLANTS

The third word is *equip*. We have accepted Jesus Christ as Savior; we have learned the Bible stories and the great movements of faith throughout human history. Now we are ready to continue stepping into the ongoing tide of God's desire for us. When I imagine the best that a congregation of any shape or size or denomination or ethnicity can be, the congregation is one where each person is able to be an active participant, supported by the leadership, to do the ministry that he or she was made to do. One of the best ways for each person to determine how he or she will participate is to understand God's intention for the person to identify and act on his or her spiritual gifts. The Natural Church Development process promotes "gift-oriented ministry" as one of the eight characteristics of healthy churches.[5] Several church movements throughout the country that are experiencing growth are talking about determining spiritual gifts as a way to plug people into ministry. Resources abound with inventories and other tools that help you find your spiritual gifts. In 0.13 seconds a Google search yielded 916,000 sites that refer to spiritual gifts. If people know their gifts, they are on their way to becoming disciples able to make a difference in the world with the good news of Jesus Christ.

There is a difference between spiritual gifts and regular talents and abilities. A spiritual gift is given for the express purpose for building up the church, or as 1 Corinthians 12 says, to help each other.

> A spiritual gift is given to each of us so we can help each other. To one person the Spirit gives the ability to give wise advice; to another the same Spirit gives a message of special knowledge. The same Spirit gives great faith to another, and to someone else the one Spirit gives the gift of healing. He gives one person the power to perform miracles, and another the ability to prophesy. He gives someone else the ability to discern whether a message is from the Spirit of God or from another spirit. Still another person is given the ability to speak in unknown languages, while another is given the ability to interpret what is being said. It is the one and only Spirit who distributes all these gifts. He alone decides which gift each person should have (vv. 7–11 NLT).

I am not going to narrowly define what the gifts are, because there are as many interpretations as there are inventories. I only want to emphasize that spiritual gifts are given to strengthen the church—God's hands and feet in the world. Sometimes they may appear as a natural talent, and so it is the way individuals use them that makes them spiritual gifts. I will use myself as an example.

Every time I take a spiritual gift inventory, two areas always rise to the top—teaching and administration. I love teaching, mainly because I love learning. I am an organized person, so I am easily able to arrange things and how they are structured. I can use these two abilities in very natural ways—keeping our home neat and organized and helping our boys learn important life lessons (they love it when I do this!). While these gifts may appear spiritual in many ways, they are true spiritual gifts when they are used to build up the church. I take advantage of many opportunities to teach in our congregation, as well as teaching and facilitating groups of pastors and laypersons through my job responsibilities as a church health specialist. Gary often shares his great ideas about wonderful things the congregation can do, and I help him map out ways to get them done. It is a win-win all the way around.

When I take a spiritual gifts inventory, a few other gifts pop up from time to time. Wisdom, knowledge, and the gift of helping behind the scenes have appeared over the years. These give me ideas of areas I can explore as I become equipped for God's service. The Holy Spirit gives these gifts for specific purposes throughout one's life. While it seems to me that God does give gifts that are central to our personalities, like administration and teaching for me, there are phases of life where God's purposes for us may change, so taking an inventory every few years may be helpful to clarifying God's desires for us as our lives change.

Being equipped for God's service by understanding and using spiritual gifts also gives us the opportunity to know what areas of service we should avoid. The spiritual gift of mercy never shows up on the top-ten list of my spiritual gifts. We have had a few laughs about this over the years, but none better than when Gary broke his ankle. He called me from the golf course, where he had "retreated" for a few days to play with his clergy buddies from the central Pennsylvania area, to let me know he had broken his ankle by sliding in the wet grass as he approached a tee set-up on a hill. He needed me to come and pick him up because he didn't think he could drive home. At the time he was about four hours away. My first reaction was, "No way! I've got work and kids in school." My second reaction—after I hung up—was, "Well, maybe I can get someone else to drive me to him, and then I can drive him and his car home." Eventually we got this worked out—but it did require the use of my organizational skills!

The doctors at the emergency room close to the golf course had put a cast on the leg and given him instructions to check in with his doctor at home. Without thinking, when we arrived at the doctor's office at home, I parked the car in such a way that we had a long walk to the door. Among other things, we learned from the doctor that Gary needed to keep his leg elevated for a significant period of time. Gary's office at that time was in our home but mine was not, so the next day I went off to work, leaving him in the recliner in the living room with his phone—but without water, without the TV remote, and all by himself. Within an hour he was calling me to bemoan his situation. I eventually got him one of those tool aprons from the hardware store so that he could put all of the essentials in the pockets and fend for himself.

We did learn a few things about spiritual gifts throughout this experience. First, don't put me in a situation where mercy is important. I am not good at hospital or shut-in visits, and I don't do well in situations that demand a lot of empathy and sympathy. I have learned to be merciful, but only for short periods of time.

The other thing that this broken ankle taught us was the way that spiritual gifts can work together. Once he began to heal from the ankle injury, Gary started to put two and two together and to fret about his future with me. Specifically, what would happen to him if he really got sick? After a long discussion about this one evening, I finally realized a solution. "Don't worry, honey. I have the gift of organization. I'll just call on everyone we know who does have a mercy gift and schedule them to come take care of you!"

For individuals, knowing their spiritual gifts is a great place to start the work of equipping. For congregations, providing opportunities for further training in hands-on ministries is important. Many congregations are training lay people in the work of caring ministries—visiting shut-ins, taking Holy Communion to people who are homebound, checking on folks that have been absent for a few weeks, and follow-up work with new guests are just a few examples. The congregations we have served incorporated spiritual gift discovery into new member classes so that these folks could identify a way to become an integral part of the congregation. A congregation that helps its participants know how they can be an active part of the ministry is a congregation that can transform its community, especially when they move on to the fourth part of the disciple-making cycle.

ENTRUSTING FAITH: HARVESTING THE FRUIT

The fourth word in this cycle of disciple making is *entrust*. Dictionary.com defines entrust as "to charge or invest with a trust or responsibility; charge with a specified office or duty involving trust."[6] In a congregation, leaders' trust of the folks who are being discipled leads to a healthy church where faith is practiced and new folks are nurtured in the faith. Jesus tried this kind of nurturing early in his ministry. He paired up the disciples and sent them out two by two to try their new skills.

> Then Jesus went from village to village, teaching the people. And he called his twelve disciples together and began sending them out two by two, giving them authority to cast out evil spirits. He told them to take nothing for their journey except a walking stick—no food, no traveler's bag, no money. He allowed them to wear sandals but not to take a change of clothes. "Wherever you go," he said, "stay in the same house until you leave town. But if any place refuses to welcome you or listen to you, shake its dust from your feet as you leave to show that you have abandoned those people to their fate." So the disciples went out, telling everyone they met to repent of their sins and turn to God. And they cast out many demons and healed many sick people, anointing them with olive oil (Mark 6:6–13 NLT).

Jesus entrusted his new disciples with what he had already established and equipped them to do. He sent them out not only to share his Father's love but also to provide a great learning experience.

My early days at Trinity United Methodist Church in Hummelstown taught me the value of entrusting by giving me responsibilities to carry my faith into the world. As a child I learned, I sang, I belonged. As a youth I learned some more, I sang some more and learned to play hand bells, I helped to lead, I went on mission trips. I was entrusted with everything I received from that congregation in order to grow up and continue my faith journey. As a young woman I grew by making decisions that were based in my faith, and when it was time to leave, that beloved congregation encouraged me to carry my faith with me wherever I went. Their trust in me has grown other disciples as I have shared my faith in Red Haw, Ohio; Austin, Pennsylvania; Graysville, Pennsylvania; Pittsburgh, Pennsylvania; Cranberry Township, Pennsylvania; and now Orlando and Winter Garden, Florida. What a great legacy for that congregation, which has sent out hundreds like me throughout its history.

Imagine a congregation where people are entrusted with their faith because they have accepted Jesus Christ as Savior, have learned about the Scriptures and the history of faithful people, and have practiced faithful living in safe and loving environments. A congregation like that could change the shape and face of its community simply by entrusting each person to do his or her part. To do this, I believe congregations need to shift their thinking. Each congregation needs to see itself as a clearinghouse for missionaries—training them up for future generations of seekers and converts. Each congregation needs to identify areas of need in its community and send people out to work within these needed areas. If all we do is learn and train for ministry but never actually meet community needs, then we are still just playing church. Establishing community ministries through which members may feed the hungry, clothe the naked, visit those in prison, and help the sick are ways laypeople are entrusted with ministry. Just imagine!

Transformation as a Cycle

I know, I know, you have heard all this before. Follow the path, run the bases, and all will be well. For the most part, people don't come to faith in neat, easy packages. John Wesley talked about prevenient grace because coming to faith can be very messy. When we look at God's involvement in each person's faith journey, somehow the messiness doesn't matter that much anymore. God is always actively calling his children to come to God. So the reality of this disciple-making cycle is that to be effective, all parts of it have to be functioning all the time. If congregations offer to evangelize but don't establish faith, they leave people hanging, and the seeds that were planted wither and die. If congregations offer to establish faith but don't equip folks for ministry, then the seeds are choked out by the thorns in people's lives. If congregations offer to equip but do not entrust folks to use their faith, then the fruit does not ripen. If congregations entrust folks to go out but they don't share their faith with others, then no new seeds are planted at all. I see this disciple-making model as a merry-go-round that never stops. People are carefully hopping on and off, or maybe some are racing along side and grabbing hold when they get a chance or diving off out of fear or frustration or simply hanging on for all the ride has to offer. What I really want to communicate to these faithful disciples, no matter where they are in the cycle, is that discipled lives influence others. Christians come to belief as individuals, our faith is established in classes and groups, we experiment with our gifts and callings in safe places, but eventually we have to move out into the world with what we have learned and experienced to interact with others.

I met a lovely older man at a training event that I was leading for a Presbyterian church several years ago. My friend and I were helping this congregation get a grip on its disciple-making process, and this gentleman was adamant that his way to share Christ with his community was by keeping his lawn neat and beautiful for everyone to enjoy. Now I could tell that he was very sincere about this, so I decided to tread carefully (remember, I have no mercy gifts). I let him talk about the care with which he does his lawn work and what a testimony he felt he was giving his community. Then I simply asked him, how does anyone know that you do this for Jesus's sake? I think he got the point. Perhaps one day a neighbor or passerby will ask him why he keeps such a lovely lawn, and, hopefully, he will be ready. I hope he now takes notice of who is around when he is outside and begins to develop a friendly relationship with them, so that when the opportunity to share his faith presents itself, he can gently share his love for God with them.

Second Peter 1 includes a passage that speaks to this very thing. I found this particular passage from Eugene Peterson's *The Message* to be particularly enlightening:

> Everything that goes into a life of pleasing God has been miraculously given to us by getting to know, personally and intimately, the One who invited us to God. The best invitation we ever received! We were also given absolutely terrific promises to pass on to you—your tickets to participation in the life of God after you turned your back on a world corrupted by lust.
>
> So don't lose a minute in building on what you have been given, complementing your basic faith with good character, spiritual understanding, alert discipline, passionate patience, reverent wonder, warm friendliness, and generous love, each dimension fitting into and developing the others. With these qualities active and growing in your lives, no grass will grow under your feet, no day will pass without its reward as you mature in your experience of our Master Jesus. Without these qualities, you can't see what is right before you, oblivious that your old sinful life has been wiped off the books.
>
> So, friends, confirm God's invitation to you, his choice of you. Don't put it off; do it now. Do this, and you'll have your life on a firm footing, the streets paved and the way wide open into the eternal kingdom of our Master and Savior, Jesus Christ.

I am totally convinced that as we imagine church, we must be bold enough to imagine the individual discipleship of *every* participant. If anything, believers must be held to a higher standard of faithful living than those who don't know Christ. But the challenge is in holding that bar higher in a loving and mature manner, not beating each other with it. We must operate with repentance and forgiveness towards each other, holding fellow Christians to faithful living. It is not okay for the church to allow Christians who exhibit poor character, little patience with others, and weak self-discipline to be examples of a Christian witness. Second Peter offers us a great stepping-stone of better behavior to exhibit to the world. Good character leads to spiritual understanding, which leads to alert (I love that word) discipline, leading to passionate patience, then reverent wonder, then warm friendliness, and finally, generous love. This is the work of disciple making. I not only want to imagine a church like that—I want to work to make it become a reality. What about you?

Reflection Questions

1. How has God's prevenient grace been evident in your life?
2. Can you look back and identify specific times when the circumstances of life provided an opportunity to be transformed?
3. Describe your church's disciple-making strategy.
4. What needs to be improved to make that strategy more fruitful?

CHAPTER 4

❧

Imagining a Bridge-Building Community of Faith

We buried my ninety-two-year-old grandmother yesterday. Nana was the matriarch of my maternal tribe. The last time I saw Nana was a little over two years ago when my father and I made a surprise visit to the skilled-care facility she resided in near Dover, Delaware. Though failing physically Nana still retained the wit and wisdom that characterized her life. When Dad and I entered her small, nondescript room and greeted her, she recognized my voice, but it took a few moments for her to figure out the face that had aged several years since my last visit. "Gary? Is that you, hon? Oh, for heaven's sake!" she exclaimed. After we embraced, Nana pointed to the wall facing her bed. "Remember?" she asked as I studied the two small oil paintings that hung in their crudely made frames. On the left was an eight-by-ten painting of a small sailboat chopping through four-foot swells on a bright, sunny day, replete with a cobalt blue sky and puffy white clouds. The painting was a Christmas gift to my grandfather, who proudly displayed it next to the front door. Now the small vessel seemed intent to sail from its framed confines into the still life hanging to its right. This much larger painting of daisies in a brass bowl I had gifted to my Nana when I was just eleven. It was the third

painting I had ever done, and I remember painting it as a birthday gift for her. The daisies hung above my grandparents' bed and
stayed there for nearly forty years. These two paintings were the
only artwork that adorned the walls of my Nana's nursing home
room. "I sit and look at them everyday—especially my daisies,"
Nana said with pride. "I show them to everyone who visits me."

At least a half dozen times during my grandmother's funeral
people came up to me to tell me how much Nana loved her daisies. The day before her passing Nana told her doctor about the
little boy who painted them for her. My cousin Karen, who was
keeping vigil with Nana, asked her, "Do you remember who that
little boy was, Nana?" "I think he was one of Alice's boys." Alice
was my mother and Nana's oldest daughter. "Yes! That's right! It
was Gary. Remember?" "Oh yes!" Nana replied. "I remember Gary
painting these for me."

As Dad and I prepared to make the long drive back from
Nana's funeral, my Uncle Paul, Nana's only son, handed me the
paintings. "I know your Nana would want you to have these back.
They brought her great joy, especially near the end." Taking them
from his hands brought me to tears—sweet tears. We never know
the depth and power our acts of love may have in another's life,
which is why we need to offer these gifts generously and as often
as possible.

I was invited by my uncle to be one of the pallbearers. When
the viewing was over, my male cousins and I walked the block
from the funeral home to St. John's Episcopal Church, the church
of our childhoods. The congregation was established back in 1728,
and the small brownstone building with the bright red front doors
accommodates around a hundred people—if they sit very close
together.

As my cousins and I stood outside the church waiting for
the hearse to arrive, one of them said, "Hey, isn't this the church
we were all baptized in?" I had been baptized in a Presbyterian
church—the one my parents were married in—across town but
had grown up in this church. "That's what I've been told, but I
don't really remember since I was just an infant at the time," my

cousin Billy shot back with a chuckle. My cousins and I quickly re-counted the number of times we had returned to St. John's Church over the past thirty years. I think the final count was three wed-dings and this funeral. Sitting together in the front pew during this celebration of my grandmother's life made me grateful to be with my Delaware tribe again and a bit nostalgic for the years we had lived only a block away from each other in Milton, Delaware. My family was the first, and only, part of the tribe to move out of state. Most of my extended family still lives close by.

As the priest directed the service, my cousins and I, now un-familiar with the Episcopal ways, fumbled through two hymnals and the Book of Common Prayer, trying to keep up with those more savvy—and failing miserably. We shot each other knowing glances and tight-lipped smiles and simply enjoyed the experience of being together in a place that had such spiritual significance for Nana and the rest of us. We were community.

Though I got the sense that my cousins have not attended wor-ship for quite some time, the church still holds an important place in their lives. They were each baptized, confirmed, and married here, as have been some of their children. Whether the experience of my Nana's funeral ever draws them back to St. John's Church, or any other church, on a more regular basis is questionable. For a brief time a connection to the church, and the faith into which they were baptized, was reestablished for them.

I tell this story because my family, like many other families the church encounters in this postmodern age, has some distant memory of more regular involvement in a community of faith. In a recent report of the Pew Forum on Religion and Public life a poll, which was based on interviews with more than thirty-five thousand Americans age eighteen and older, found that religious affiliation in the United States is rapidly changing.

More than one-quarter of American adults (28 percent) have left the faith in which they were raised in favor of another religion—or no religion at all. If change in affiliation from one type of Protestantism to another is included, 44 percent of adults have either switched religious affiliation, moved from being

unaffiliated with any religion to being affiliated with a particular
faith, or dropped any connection to a specific religious tradition
altogether. The survey finds that the number of people who say
they are unaffiliated with any particular faith today (16.1 percent)
is more than double the number who say they were not affiliated
with any particular religion as children. Among Americans ages
eighteen to twenty-nine, one in four say they are not.[1]

While the unaffiliated still carry some sense of the church's
significance in their lives—mainly through rites and rituals like
baptisms, weddings, and funerals—they are rapidly becoming
disconnected from it. Observing how my cousins struggled with
the liturgy of my grandmother's funeral accentuated the disconnect I sensed between them and the organized church. Even I, an
ordained minister in another denomination, found myself getting
frustrated trying to follow along. A simple thing like the priest
taking the time to explain what we were doing and why it was
important would have been helpful. When we were asked to follow along on a particular page, knowing which particular book—
and there were three of them in the pew racks in front of us—he
was referring to would have been useful. He assumed incorrectly
that we were all "churched" people and therefore could follow
along. While his homily was—in my humble opinion—biblically
grounded and theologically sound, it lacked energy or any attempt
to include us. The priest seemed to be simply going through the
motions of the service while we sat there numbly as spectators.

Who Locked the Gates?

In my ongoing conversations with people who have tried, and
failed, to get through the gates of the church, I have heard painful stories of how they couldn't get past the unspoken codes and
requirements those of us "inside" the church unwittingly embody
and construct as barriers toward them—including unspoken
dress codes, being made to feel like intruders by the members of
the church, the expectation that they should be familiar with our

creeds and prayers (I can't tell you how many churches I visit that never print these in a bulletin or project them on a screen for folks to follow), and being inundated by words and expressions (church speak), especially in our sermons, that presuppose some greater theological knowledge and experience of the church than they really have.

I recently visited a new church trying to get established in our community. As a church planter I am always interested in how other new church starts are getting established and make it a point to visit these new churches as often as I can. The service at this particular church was held in an elementary school cafeteria. I arrived ten minutes before worship to poke around a bit. Five minutes before the service was to begin I settled into my seat. I waited another twenty-five minutes after the advertised start time until someone in the church's band finally said, from the back of the room, "I guess we ought to get started." The pastor's message went on for nearly an hour and focused on the "frequency and complexity of covenants throughout the Bible." Ten minutes into his message and I was planning my exit strategy. Had it not been for the families on either side of me blocking me in my seat, I would have bolted for the door. My own experience of visiting with other churches has helped me realize what a huge step it is for "unaffiliated" people—the ones we say we are trying to reach—to show up especially on Sunday mornings and find their place among us. It has got to be about as uncomfortable for many of them to come and feel connected to what we are doing as it would be for us churched folk to show up at a Hindu shrine and jump right into the ritual.

Many of the unaffiliated people I relate to on a weekly basis would be open to visiting a church but often need an entry point like a baptism, wedding, or funeral to do so. I have found over and over again that these occasions can create opportunities for us to connect with the unaffiliated—to build a bridge to where they are. Again, I believe it is *our* responsibility as clergy and laity to build these bridges to *them*. As they begin to join us in the journey, we can then lead them to begin to take responsibility for themselves—to understand about our history, to study our traditions, to learn how to spiritually feed themselves. But the process begins with us in the church.

I am alarmed by the number of my clergy colleagues who respond antagonistically toward unaffiliated people who these pastors say "just want to use us" when they turn to the church with a need—be it a baptism, wedding, or funeral. My church-planting experience has shown me that these life events become incredible opportunities to build relationships with the unaffiliated. As an ordained clergy member of the church, I *do* require a prebaptism counseling session for families who want to have their children baptized. I have been trained to provide premarital counseling sessions and make this a part of my ministry with couples who want to get married by me—whether in the church, in a park, or on a beach. When I am officiating a funeral for families—unaffiliated or otherwise—I make it a point to spend a significant amount of time with them before and after the service. This is really just good pastoral ministry. And I have never had an unaffiliated family come to me for a baptism, wedding, or funeral and decide not to use my "services" because I wanted to spend time with them. On the contrary, most of these families have been pleasantly surprised at the amount of time I have been willing to invest in their lives. Every church I have served has grown numerically by these encounters.

I think we have a huge problem when unaffiliated people turn to our churches for services and support and we respond to them in a way that conveys a kind of club mentality that says, "If you are not a member here, attend regularly, or support 'us' financially, your request for services will be denied or at least met with lengthy policies and hefty fees." Such a response sends the message, "It's not about you. *We're* not about you!"

But who or what are we about?

In my thirty years of ministry I have watched the chasm between the church and our culture widen considerably. As leaders in the church, we are much too quick to place the blame for this on those outside of our faith communities: "If only *they* would come to us . . . If only *they* would place *their* butts in our seats . . . If only *they* would put *their* generous contributions in our collection plates . . . If only *they* . . . there would be no chasm between us." Not so fast. If only *we* would go to be where *they* are . . . If only *we* would listen to *their* concerns . . . If only *we* would be attentive to *their* needs . . . If only *we* would stop treating people as a means to *our* ends. (How many times have I heard people in the church say, "Our financial problems would be over if we could only get more people in the seats"!) It is not that people aren't spiritually minded these days. Studies have shown that while church attendance is declining in North America, interest in spirituality is increasing. So, where is the disconnect? As a leader in the church, I had better be asking this question a lot—of myself and my church.

In his book *The Present Future*, Reggie McNeal, author and missional leadership specialist for Leadership Network of Dallas, Texas, writes, "People may be turned off by the church, but they are not turned off by Jesus. Church people sometimes get excited by this but fail to understand that people in the non-church culture don't associate Jesus with the church. In their minds the church is a club for religious people where club members can celebrate their traditions and hang out with others who share common thinking and lifestyles."[2] While we can expect clubs to provide services exclusively to their members—that is what the members pay for—the church is different. Because of the Great Commission and the Great Commandment, service to others is something we who are already in the church pay for. While club members legitimately have a "serve us" mentality, church members should have a "service" mentality. When we first started HopeSpring Church I talked about this in one of my sermons. That week a member made a sign for my office. "The church is the only organization that exists for its nonmembers." My own experience in ministry has confirmed—more times than I would like to admit—that McNeal is right.

Years ago I read Kennon Callahan's book *Effective Church Leadership* in which he states, "The day of the professional minister is over. The day of the missionary pastor has come."[3] At the time, I missed Callahan's point. As a classically trained "ministry professional," I was too caught up in my own gatekeeper style of leadership. I was hired to care for the flock already inside the gates and to make sure nothing got at them (including the stinging truth of the gospel). My prayer is that the Holy Spirit breaks through my own propensity toward a gatekeeper approach of ministry to consider, again and again, another way—a more bridge-building way.

Dreaming of a Better Way

The first significant crack came right out of seminary when I was appointed by the bishop to serve a three-point circuit in the Appalachian communities of north central Pennsylvania. The logging industry—once booming in these now impoverished communities—had been completely wiped out by a flood in 1912. At one time the two-mile-long lumber mill was the largest in the world. Without it the area fell into and remained in economic hardship. Though attempts were made to revitalize the area, it never recovered. Even in the mideighties, when Kim and I were living there, there was little work for people. Addiction, violence, and poverty hung over the community like a dark, impenetrable cloud. It was the roughest, rowdiest, and scariest place I had ever been. The people of the area were clannish, rugged, and brutally honest.

In the United Methodist church, clergy are appointed to their ministries by a bishop based on the needs of the local church and the particular gifts and graces of the pastor—at least that is the way it is supposed to work. I learned later that I was appointed to this parish because there was no other place for me to go. Early on in my appointment I had to make the decision to be a bridge builder rather than a gatekeeper. A dream I had soon after my appointment solidified this for me. In my dream I was sitting on the front steps of the church. Steady streams of people were passing by. Most of them were bent over, disfigured, and dressed in rags— men, women, and children alike. As they passed by, they turned toward me and I noticed each one had the same face—the face of

Jesus. I didn't want to serve in this parish. I had never lived in a place of such poverty. I *was required to be* there because the bishop said so, but I didn't *want* to be there—until this dream. Then we fell in love with them.

The largest of the three churches I served had about forty people attending worship on Sunday morning. My smallest church had eight. With the exception of an elderly Catholic priest who would drive in from a nearby community to lead Mass on Sunday mornings, I was the only resident pastor in the entire southern part of the county. Because I served a parish of predominately older people, I had a lot of funerals. After the first six or seven of these, family members—outside the church—who had attended one of the funerals began to ask me to lead funerals for their loved ones. By my second year I was averaging twenty-seven funerals a year. Most of these were for "unaffiliated" folks. I decided I would serve these families as if they were members of my church. In the six years of my ministry there, worship attendance grew from 40 to 120 people. We averaged twenty to thirty new professions of faith each year. Because we filled every space we could find in the church for small groups and Sunday school classes, our parsonage next door became the church annex. By our sixth year the church was filled with young families and lots of children.

When the bishop decided to visit every congregation in the Central Pennsylvania Conference (which, I believe, involved more than six hundred churches) he stopped at our church, listened to our story, and marveled at the transformation we had experienced. When he asked what was the most significant thing I had done as a pastor to encourage this growth I responded, "Funeral evangelism." I let the funeral director know that I was willing to conduct funerals for families without a church home. I asked the women of the church—who loved to cook—to provide meals for these families in our modest fellowship hall. I coordinated visits between some of our leaders gifted with care and compassion and the families of the deceased. I watched our small, struggling church grow numerically and financially through death.

Bridge builders find ways to extend God's love from the church into the community. Gatekeepers find ways to keep the community from coming into the church.

Breaking Down the Gates

I stepped into my first experience as a pastor at the ripe old age of eighteen. A dying inner-city congregation needed a part-time pastor. I wanted to test my calling and gain some ministry experience while attending college, so when this dying congregation was offered to me I jumped at the chance. "What could I possibly do to make things worse?" I thought to myself.

White flight to the suburbs had decimated this urban congregation, stranding a handful of elderly widows who did not have the wherewithal to flee from their homes like everyone else. These wonderful women immediately adopted me. I would arrive at the church after morning classes only to be fought over by two of the women who lived on opposite corners from the church. "It's my turn to have him over for lunch. You had him last week!" Eventually, one of them would concede to the other, and I would soon be sitting pretty in front of a plate of delicious food. Those were great years for me personally because I was *their* pastor—I was in *their* church and therefore was well cared for. I did my best to care for the members of this church but felt my ministry ought also to have an outreaching component to it.

I knew being a pastor meant caring for the people of this congregation but I also sensed it meant much more than that. I was pretty sure I was supposed to be out in the community getting to know people so that I could invite them into our church. Without any help from the members of the church (which was not a good idea—I see now that this should have been a partnership), I would go door to door and personally invite people to our church— black people, Jewish people, gay people, single mothers, couples of mixed race—they all mattered to me because I believed they mattered to God. I developed relationships with some of these neighbors. Eventually a few of them would show up in worship; but, in spite of my warm welcome *out there*, they were treated coldly by the members *in here*. Some of the elders of the church made it known to my "other than old, straight, white, married, or widowed friends" that they were not welcome here. There were churches for their types elsewhere. Gatekeeper churches tend to shut and lock the gate toward those who are not like them.

During my personal outreach to the community I noticed a large number of children and youth playing in the streets. Our church had a beautiful basement furnished with ping-pong tables and a shuffleboard inlayed in the tile floor. The older members of the church rarely ventured down to the basement and so it was largely unused. I decided (without approval from the board) to open the basement on Friday nights so that the kids of the city could come in off the streets to play or just hang out. I was eventually told I couldn't continue doing this because the kids might scuff the floor or dirty the walls. Gatekeepers tend to be more concerned about their facilities than facilitating ministries in their communities.

A local neighborhood center desperately needed room to store clothing and household items for monthly distribution in our area. They approached the leadership of the church, asking if they could utilize one of the six empty classrooms in the educational wing. The church leadership, at one of its monthly meetings, determined its classrooms were not intended for that purpose and therefore declined to help.

Gatekeepers aren't confined to our cities. During seminary I served a small rural church nestled among twenty houses at a country crossroad, an asphalt X marked through acres and acres of cornfields. The sixty members of the church were close-knit, caring, deeply religious, set in their ways, and all related—in some fashion. They were some of the most generous people we have ever met and to this day are some of our dearest friends. Early in their journey they were an outreaching community of faith, but somewhere along the way they had become gatekeepers. This was especially evident at one board meeting when we were celebrating a community outreach event we had just sponsored to help a neighbor in need. A local man had suffered a horrible stroke that left him in a rehabilitation center sixty miles away from his home for nearly a year. His wife became the sole provider for her household, which included a teenage son. They were not members of our church, but someone shared them as a prayer concern during worship. Conversations about the family ensued after the service as people questioned what our church might do to help them. Someone suggested we organize a benefit chili supper to raise money for the family. The entire room buzzed with energy and ideas. Since chili is one of the few things I can cook—and that very well—I made a pot to bring, and so did a dozen others. We advertised the event locally as well as in neighboring towns. To our surprise nearly two hundred people came, ate our chili, and donated generously to the cause. In this two-hour event our little church raised nearly three thousand dollars. It was amazing!

At our next board meeting the excitement over what we had done was still bubbling. Someone suggested we do it again for someone else in need. A divorced young mother of three, just down the road, was battling breast cancer. With medical bills mounting, she didn't know how she would be able to care for her children. "Why don't we sponsor a supper for her?" "Yeah, we could do a spaghetti dinner this time!" More ideas flowed around the table. And then a voice asked, "When do we stop? Where's the end to this? I mean, we did it for one family and now we're talking about doing it for another. When is enough—enough?" I watched as the buzzing stopped and conversation took a 180-degree turn. Soon, the very people who had been tossing out ideas for outreach were shooting those same ideas full of holes. The "needs" of the church (mainly its building) took center stage, and by the end of the evening all plans to sponsor another dinner had ceased and a motion was made and passed to raise money for a new entranceway to the church. (Wow! As I was writing this just now, the irony of that one struck me.)

Gatekeepers do that. They open the door widely for people like themselves and bar it shut from those who are needy, different, or just plain make them feel uncomfortable. They don't realize that in doing so, they are keeping people from experiencing and growing in their relationship with God. I eventually stopped inviting people to my city church. It was doing far more harm than good. People showing a genuine interest in the church were met by folks who were genuinely disinterested in them. I fought to keep the country church focused on its community and from time to time made a little headway. Gatekeeper churches will break God's heart because this is the same God who broke down the gates of sin that divided us from him by sending his only Son into the world to build a bridge to us. Bridge-builder churches embody this very nature of God.

The church is well on its way to extinction—or at least complete irrelevance—if it does not become more intentional about extending itself outward into the community. As a church-planting pastor, I understand the importance of this outward orientation because, when you are starting a church from scratch, you cannot thrive unless you understand the demographics of your target area and are willing to go where the people are and meet them at the place of *their* need. If the new churches I am helping start were to begin in a gatekeeper mode, they would not survive their first year. Unlike new churches, existing churches *can* survive for a time without this outward impetus—if they have endowments, a few loyal followers, and a reasonably good worship service that keeps the current folks coming. But without an outward orientation their demise is just a matter of time. Unfortunately, such is the downfall of thousands and thousands of churches in my own denomination, many of which are already on some form of hospice care. Escalating costs for staffing, insurances, and facility maintenance alone are pushing some of these churches over the edge. The Florida Conference, in which I serve, will take the assets of these churches when they close and invest the money in new church starts or a consulting process that will help existing congregations re-vision and refocus their ministry. My ministry is focused on new church starts, and Kim's is focused on revitalizing existing churches. Together we are committed to helping every church move from *survive* to *thrive*. In our experience, we believe only those churches that make the shift from gatekeeper to bridge builder will experience fruitfulness in this postmodern world.

Practicing Radical Hospitality

The Greek word for hospitality in the New Testament is *philoxenia*. It literally means "love of stranger" (*philo* = love; *xeno* = stranger). Someone who is xenophobic has a fear of strangers. Philoxenia, or hospitality, requires more than providing first-time guests with coffee and donuts on Sunday morning—although our first-timers comment on how much they love this! Philoxenia has to do with making others feel comfortable. It has everything to do with the attitude and the spirit with which we convey a sense of genuine acceptance of those who are not like us.

In the book of Leviticus, Moses instructs the children of Israel on the treatment of aliens in their midst ("aliens" meaning not ET and his friends but people outside their community, strangers, foreigners, non-Jews). "When an alien resides with you in your land, you shall not oppress the alien. The alien who resides with you shall be to you as the citizen among you; you shall love the alien as yourself, for you were aliens in the land of Egypt" (Lev. 19:33–34 NRSV). God's people, the Hebrews, once knew what it had been like to be aliens while in captivity in Egypt and Babylonia. God wanted them to remember that experience and understand how important it was for them to practice philoxenia—to genuinely welcome those who were strangers in their midst. We understand, through the incarnation of Christ, that God—the Chief Bridge Builder—desires a relationship with all humankind. God expects the church—also the incarnation of Christ in the world— to practice philoxenia. To do this means we have to confront some of the prejudices we have against others because of race, economic status, color, beliefs, and sexual orientation.

Kim and I were challenged by an opportunity we had not only to personally practice philoxenia toward someone very different from us but also to model philoxenia for the church we served. We met Bob Morris during our pastorate in the Appalachian Mountains of north-central Pennsylvania. In the town of Austin, where we lived, families tended to group themselves among their kin in the hollers and backwoods of the area. Bob and his wife, Peggy, both in their early fifties, had visited our church once and, because they were dressed poorly and lacked proper hygiene, had received a cold reception from our people. I am ashamed to say I remember being one of the persons repulsed by their appearance and odor. The Morrises lived in a rundown house way back in one of the hollers on the outskirts of town. Because Bob had mental and physical disabilities, Peggy had full responsibility for their well-being.

I was in the office working on my sermon when a funeral director friend of mine, Tom, called and requested that I come to his office as soon as possible. An ongoing battle with diabetes and heart disease ended Peggy's life. Now that she was gone, Bob was left to care for himself—something he had never done before.

When I entered Tom's office the first thing I noticed was the awful stench—and not the kind you might expect in a funeral home. Tom greeted me and filled me in on the details—no next of kin, no money for a funeral, no means of support, nothing. Bob was alone in the world and did not have the ability to care for himself. As Tom directed me to the room where Bob was waiting, the stench grew stronger, eventually leading me to its source. Bob was sitting bent over with his head between his hands. "Mr. Morris, this is Reverend Shockley, the pastor I was telling you about. He lives in your neighborhood and is here to help you." Bob slowly raised his head. He looked at least ten years older than he really was—fifty-five. His oily salt and pepper hair was matted to his head. His face had not seen a razor in days. His clothes were worn and soiled. He had a glass eye that remained fixed as he looked around the room, eventually setting his sight on me. Extending my right hand, I said, "Mr. Morris, I'm sorry about your loss. I want to do whatever I can to help you." Tom volunteered to care for the expense of Peggy's cremation. There would be no formal service since Bob had no next of kin or friends. The greatest question remained, however: "What do we do with Bob?"

I had dealt with homeless people before. Usually they would drop by the church looking for food or money. The city church I served always had a supply of food on hand that I could give them, although I made it a practice never to hand out cash. Bob wasn't exactly homeless, and he wasn't looking for food or money.

I needed some time to think about the situation and, since Bob was unable to care for himself, decided to take him home with me. In a ploy to clean him up and get rid of his smelly clothes, I said to Bob on the way to my house, "You know what always makes me feel better when I'm upset about something? I take a nice hot bath." Bob said that sounded like a good idea. While he was bathing I took his clothes out back and burned them. I was at least a foot taller and fifty pounds heavier than Bob, so the clothes I gave him from my wardrobe were long and baggy, but I rolled up his sleeves and pant legs so that he wouldn't trip coming down the steps. I made Bob some hot tea and invited him to relax on the couch. Kim was still at work and had no idea any of this was happening in her home. Looking back, I probably should have called to warn her. Of course, she was very friendly and hospitable toward Bob and agreed that he should stay with us until we could figure out his next steps. She told me I was responsible for removing the ring from the tub.

In the days that followed Peggy's death, I contacted multiple social service agencies to seek help for Bob. I learned that in addition to the welfare he had been receiving, his mental disabilities qualified him for residence in a group home. The problem was that no spaces were available for him. While we waited for a spot to open for Bob, the Austin Church quickly mobilized to help us care for Bob. We decided to have a memorial service for Peggy. Nearly fifty people from our congregation came and stayed for the luncheon prepared by our women's group. Packages of clothing appeared on our front porch, as did home-cooked meals to help us feed our guest.

In spite of our good care, Bob wanted to go back to his own home just a few blocks from our parsonage. We felt this would be okay as long as we had people who would stop by to check on him, cook his meals, and keep his place clean, but we decided we should make sure the house was suitable for Bob's return. I will never forget when a small group of us from the church first stepped into Bob's home. It was the filthiest place we had ever seen. I don't think I can describe it here without gagging. After a crew spent several days of cleaning—and burning the stuff that could not be cleaned—Bob returned to his home.

The first few nights back at his place went fairly well until it was my turn to stop by with dinner. As I approached his home, I smelled smoke. Through the kitchen window I could see flames coming from an electric frying pan. I rushed inside, opened the kitchen window, and tossed the frying pan—flames and all—out into the yard. Bob was sound asleep on the couch. When he awoke to discover what I had done, he became furious with me. How dare I come into his house and ruin his dinner like that!

Some of us from the church tried to help Bob find a cleaner place to live where he would also be supervised until the group home became available, but we were unsuccessful, and so we stepped up our visits with Bob while he continued to live in his own home. We arranged for people to make and bring meals to Bob each day and found some volunteers from the church who would help keep up with the cleaning. Finally, after several weeks of this intensive caregiving, Bob was accepted into a facility in Coudersport, ten miles north of our community.

About a year later Kim and I were walking along Main Street in Coudersport when a well-dressed man in a coat and tie holding the hand of a woman about the same age came toward us. It wasn't until he was closer, and I noticed the glass eye and familiar crooked smile, that I recognized it was Bob Morris. We stopped and chatted for a few minutes. Bob introduced us to his girlfriend and shared how much he liked his new home. He thanked us profusely for all the kindness we had shown him. Bob was indeed a new man.

I wish this story had a happier ending, but we learned a short time after this visit with Bob that he had been struck by a car and killed outside his home. Before his death, however, Bob had discovered everything he had ever wanted—love, acceptance, friendship, and shelter. And through Bob we learned the value of building a bridge to someone who on the outside appeared vastly different from us but on the inside is still very much the same— a beloved child of God seeking a place in this world to belong. Radical hospitality compels us to build bridges beyond our gates to extend the love and presence of God to those with whom we would otherwise not associate.

Working for Social Justice

Philoxenia requires the church to build bridges that extend the friendship of God out into the wider world. Peter Storey, former bishop of the Johannesburg-Soweto, South Africa, area and national leader of the Methodist Church of Southern Africa, writes in his book *Listening at Golgotha*:

> It seems that if we want to come near to this Christ, we must follow him in being among those we would not always want to associate with. Some tell us that following Jesus is a simple matter of inviting him into our hearts. But when we do that, Jesus always asks, "May I bring my friends?" And when we look at them, we see that they are not the kind of company we like to keep. The friends of Jesus are the outcasts, the marginalized, the poor, the homeless, the rejected—the lepers of life. We hesitate and ask, "Jesus, must we really have them too?" Jesus replies, "Love me, love my friends."[4]

It seems to me that if I truly want to experience the presence of Jesus and *be* the presence of Jesus in the wider world, many avenues are available for me to take—and one of them is to be among the poor. I have found that Jesus has a strange way of staring back at me every time I look into the eyes of someone in desperate need.

I recently completed a sermon series entitled "Encountering God in the Old Testament." It was the first time I ever spent this much time preaching on the first half of the Bible. Apparently I am not the only one who has shied away from doing so. I received more comments on this series from folks than on any sermons I have ever done. I enjoyed delving into the ancient texts *until* I preached on, and became convicted by, the prophets, and especially the prophet Isaiah. He wrote:

> When you come to worship me, who asked you to parade through my courts with all your ceremony? Stop bringing me your meaningless gifts; the incense of your offerings disgusts me! As for your celebrations of the new moon and the Sabbath and your special days for fasting—they are all sinful and false. I want no more of your pious meetings. I hate your new moon celebrations and your annual festivals. They are a burden to me. I cannot stand them! When you lift up your hands in prayer, I will not look. Though you offer many prayers, I will not listen, for your hands are covered with the blood of innocent victims. Wash yourselves and be clean! Get your sins out of my sight. Give up your evil ways. Learn to do good. Seek justice. Help the oppressed. Defend the cause of orphans. Fight for the rights of widows (Isa. 1:12–17 NLT).

What breaks your heart? The heart of your church? Do you care about God's least, last, and lost children—enough to be bothered in your sleep? Enough to be stirred from your comfort and complacency? Enough to act?

Quite some time ago I was preaching on social justice issues and how, as Christians, we tend to want to hide from the needs of others in order to maintain our own comfort and complacency. I shared this quote I found attributed to Wilbur Reese: "I would like to buy $3 worth of God please. Not enough to explode my soul or disturb my sleep, but just enough to equal a cup of warm milk or a snooze in the sunshine. I don't want enough of Him to make me love a black man or pick beets with a migrant worker. I want ecstasy, not transformation; I want the warmth of the womb, not a new birth. I want a pound of the Eternal in a paper sack. I would like to buy $3 worth of God, please."[5] Only when we learn to set our own needs aside and take up the cause of building bridges to help meet the needs of others do we truly experience new birth and spiritual transformation.

It's Really Not about Me . . . or You

I grew up in a church that taught me Jesus died to save me from my sins, to fill me with the Holy Spirit, to grant me eternal life in heaven when I die. I grew up believing that my response to God for all this was to go to church, read the Bible, pray, and tell other people about Jesus. This egocentric distortion of the gospel was challenged when I served a church in the red-light district of the inner city, the impoverished Appalachian Mountain communities of north central Pennsylvania, and now central Florida where, in the land of the "worlds"—like Disney World and Sea World—human need and suffering get hidden behind fantasy and illusion.

Just recently I read that there are 140 makeshift tent villages in central Florida alone that house thousands of homeless men, women and children. On average, 250,000 to 350,000 migrant workers pick citrus in Florida and earn eight thousand dollars or less per household annually. More than two thousand migrant children lack sufficient health care and education. These children have no choice but to stay in the fields while their families work. Sadly, hundreds of these children get injured each year. Learning these things about my own mission field has shattered my once myopic vision of Christianity being all about me, and I am left to struggle now with what I see.

I recently got a new pair of glasses. I like them, not only because they have stylish black frames but also because the progressive lenses enable me to see things a lot more clearly. In many ways it would have been easier to keep the old lenses that ever so slightly blurred my view of the world around me. At least then I would have had an excuse for not seeing things as clearly as I could have. Now I have no excuse. We know that true vision isn't something that begins with the eye—it starts in the heart—and then shapes the ability of the eyes to see. I think this is what Jesus meant when he chastised some of the religious leaders of his day who questioned his ability to heal a man who had been blind from birth. These leaders may have had 20/20 physical vision but were spiritually blind nonetheless. "Jesus said, 'I came into this world for judgment so that those who do not see may see, and those who do see may become blind.' Some of the Pharisees near him heard this and said to him, 'Surely we are not blind, are we?' Jesus said to them, 'If you were blind, you would not have sin. But now that you say, "We see," your sin remains'" (John 9:39–41 NRSV).

I am personally praying for a new vision of what it means to be the church, a sharper vision of my own heart that will help me see people, including the migrant workers and homeless men, women, and children, who have otherwise remained hidden from my sight. And I pray for more sleepless nights, a restlessness of the soul, a holy discontent that will continue to draw me nearer to God and at the same time push me farther away from myself into a world that waits and hopes for churches like mine and people like me to build bridges.

I gave my Nana's painting of the daisies to Kim to hang in her office. It is a way of extending my love for my grandmother to my wife, whom I love with all my heart and who hasn't received a Shockley original in a long, long time. I seem to have less and less time these days for painting pictures that hang on walls, though. Kim and I seem to spending more and more of our time helping the church to envision a picture of what it means to get outside of itself and build bridges that will extend love and grace to a world that, in many ways, has lost a sense of God's vision for it and increasingly only sees chaos, loneliness, and pain. Get out of your gates and join us. I am not sure the world can live without us!

Reflection Questions

1. How do leaders in the church you serve function as gatekeepers? What specific behaviors are evidence of this?

2. Respond to Reggie McNeal's statement, "People may be turned off by the church, but they are not turned off by Jesus." Do you think this is true? Why or why not?

3. Who are the people most in need of the ministry of your church? What are some ways you could build a bridge to them?

4. How does your church practice philoxenia?

5. What causes you, and your church, sleepless nights, a restlessness of the soul, a holy discontent?

CHAPTER 5

⌒

Imagining Worship as Thin Space

The church I serve as pastor has a ten-year partnership with a Methodist Church situated on the peace lines in Belfast, and I have been privileged to travel to Northern Ireland twice in the past two years. In addition to being richly blessed by the numerous friendships I have made during these visits, I find my faith has been profoundly affected by the ancient spirituality of the land. The landscape of Northern Ireland is dotted by monuments and ancient ruins reminding all who visit them that this is holy ground where people long ago experienced something spiritually significant and found themselves transformed. I have experienced such graced moments of transformation in my own spiritual journey, and my pilgrimages to Northern Ireland have given me a new language in which to describe them. The ancient pre-Christian and Celtic people referred to these transformational experiences simply as "thin spaces." Short, sweet—but fully descriptive. These early cultures embraced thin spaces as moments and places when the veil between this world and the "other world" is suddenly *thinned*.

I first experienced one of these thin spaces in Northern Ireland when I visited the remnants of an eleventh-century Cistercian monastery called Inch Abbey. Typically the weather in Ireland in mid-September is cold and rainy, but this day was warm and sunny. As I walked among the ruins, I felt myself being drawn into a thin space. I lost all sense of time. The weariness I had been feeling from my flights the day before gave way to an absolute sense of relaxation and peace. Everything around me somehow seemed *more* real. Colors were more vibrant and the scents in the air more pungent. All of my senses seemed more fully attuned to the moment. God somehow seemed nearer, as did the people who had once occupied this place. I sat quietly surveying the gray stone remnants of the abbey and the lush green fields around us. About a hundred yards off to the west was a centuries-old cemetery. Half a mile to the east, across a shimmering lake, was a four-hundred-year-old church still in use today. In my mind's eye I imagined the men of the abbey going about their disciplined tasks—toiling in gardens, eating together, worshiping in the sanctuary, chanting praises to God.

I have always prided myself in having a vivid imagination, but this thin space experience at the abbey seemed so much more than that. I felt oddly aware of past and present together—like the times I feel spiritually connected to my mother, who is deceased, whenever I eat pineapple upside-down cake or decorate the house for Christmas. Or the connection I feel with my deceased mother-and father-in-law when I am toiling in the garden or celebrating the birthdays of their grandsons. At Inch Abbey I found my whole self, along with the hearts and voices that once extolled God in this place so long ago, lifted up in praise and adoration of God: "O LORD, our Lord, your majestic name fills the earth! Your glory is higher than the heavens" (Ps. 8:1 NLT).

One of my friends on the trip was an artist who came prepared with paper and watercolors. I had brought a sketchpad and pencils but inadvertently left them in the hotel. When Peg realized I had none of my supplies, she quickly found a sketchpad and some drawing pencils for me. I perched myself atop the remains of a column that once supported the roof of the nave and gave myself fully to this thin space. For the next hour, which seemed to pass in a mere minute, I squinted and sketched and basked in the sun. For the remainder of my trip I spent each evening refining my drawing and complementing it with watercolor. I was sitting in the Belfast airport waiting to board the plane for home when I added the last bit of detail to the piece. It hangs near the front entrance of our home. It is a treasure. Thin spaces are graced moments and places when God's Spirit meets us and invites us to journey deeper into the community of faith. In thin spaces spiritual seekers from the past join with us as we journey with God in the present. There is biblical precedence for this connectedness. I am reminded of thin space moments like that on the Mount of Transfiguration, where people from the present—Jesus, Peter, James, and John— suddenly find themselves standing alongside people from the past, Moses and Elijah. The experience of that thin space was so powerful the disciples of Jesus wanted to box it up and keep it for later. I think they wanted to hold on to it tightly for fear that such a thin space might never avail itself again. Thin spaces, or mountaintop experiences, as we sometimes call them, can be so life affirming and life changing that we don't want to let go of them either. Not wanting my experience at Inch Abbey to end that September day, I stayed immersed in the experience as long as I could until the rest of the group insisted it was time to move on.

The Relational Nature of Worship as Thin Space

We don't have to travel halfway around the world to experience thin spaces. The distance between "here" and "there" can be spanned even in the ordinary places of our lives. For me thin spaces almost always incorporate these elements: a sense of community past, present, and future; an environment that promotes awareness of God's transcendence; and, of course, my openness to the experience. When these elements are working together, I can experience a thin space whether sitting quietly in a sanctuary, lifting my hands in praise to God in the middle-school cafeteria where our new church gathers for worship, sitting next to a trout stream, strolling through a forest, watching the sun set with a friend, abiding with a parishioner as she takes her last breath, or chatting with my teenage son about issues of life and faith.

Thin spaces remind us *this* is not all there is and we are *not* alone. Thin spaces are unique opportunities to pause, consider, and even imagine what lies beyond our everyday lives. They invade the very core of our human heart and create in us a hunger and yearning common to all God's people—the hunger to be connected, to become a part of something greater, to be loved, to be accepted, to find peace. St. Augustine, maybe out of the experience of his own thin places, wrote this beautiful prayer: "and our heart is restless until it find rest in you."[1]

Think how much healthier planning and leading of worship would be if church leaders approached each of these experiences as potential thin spaces. What a difference it would make if we gathered in the fullness of the Divine more keenly aware of a faith community that encompasses past, present, and future. My thin space experience at Inch Abbey heightened my awareness of people of faith from the past, acknowledged my church family in the present, and reminded me that someday—when I am gone—others will take my place. Right now, we live in a stream of faithful people who have run with endurance the race that God set before them (Heb. 12:1b). Thin places are all about connection—with God and with all who have lived, are living, and will live in generations to come. Thin spaces remind us that we simultaneously inherit, inhabit, and entrust to each other the faith that has been passed on to us by those who have, or still are, journeying with God. Worship as a thin space heightens my awareness of this faith continuum that is bridged and held together by the omnipresent God. The relational nature of worship as thin space means that worship points us in different directions: from us to God, from God to us, from us to us.

FROM US TO GOD

In my formative days in the church, my worship experience was mostly a vertical one—from *me to God*. God was the audience or recipient of my worship. Everything around me—statues, stained glass windows, candles, vestments, and other accoutrements—lifted my eyes and heart above the mundane and ordinariness of life to consider the majesty, holiness, and awesomeness of God. I believed God waited for me to enter the sanctuary to act out my faith through prayer, song, and sacrament. Everything I did and said during the service pointed my mind and heart toward God. In this way worship was essentially my performance *for* God. Søren Kierkegaard, the nineteenth-century Danish philosopher, suggested you and I are the primary actors in the drama of worship. The clergy, organist, choir, and ushers are the supporting cast. And God, according to Kierkegaard, is the audience. The way we pray, sing songs of praise, offer our money, and attend to Scripture and sermon all contribute to our worship performance before God. Everything we do in worship is directed *toward* the Divine. In the early days of my pastoral ministry, I often referred to worship as having an audience of One and would remind myself, and the congregation's worship leaders, that our primary task was to direct the congregation toward God. Though my understanding and practice of worship has expanded beyond the "me to God" direction, I still find myself wondering on most Sunday afternoons if God was pleased with what *I* did that day.

FROM GOD TO US

For many of us, worship can be described as more of a *God to me* experience. Worship is seen as the opportunity to gather with the community of faith to *receive* something from God. We come to receive the sacraments, to hear a good sermon, to receive prayer and anointing oil for healing. We come to be uplifted, motivated, comforted, and reminded that God is *with* and *for* us. I know when people have received something from the experience of worship when they say things like, "Your sermon really spoke to me this morning" or "I really liked the music today—you sang some of my favorite songs" or "I felt comforted during the prayer time" or "I felt moved by my experience of communion this week!" There is nothing wrong with wanting to receive something from worship. It would be unrealistic to expect otherwise, since we enter worship as little children with our hands held out, hoping for our Divine Parent to meet our needs. I think this is actually a wonderful image for us, but by itself, it is limited.

My mother (a former Roman Catholic) and I used to argue about whether children should be allowed to receive the sacrament of Holy Communion. As United Methodists, my family and the congregations I have served celebrate an open table, which means we offer the sacraments to whomever desires them—including children. People do not need to be members of our church or any church for that matter. They only need to come with open hands. My mother, however, believed a person should be confirmed before receiving communion. She felt a child would not have the appreciation nor the understanding to receive this sacrament.

When my son was about two, she and my father were visiting us one weekend when the small, rural congregation I was serving celebrated its monthly communion service. Kim was playing the piano for worship that morning—one of the fringe benefits the church received when they hired me. I stood in the center aisle, tearing off a piece of the bread and serving it to each communicant with the words, "This is the body of Christ." A layperson, Sue, standing next to me, extended the cup, and as each person dipped the bread in the juice, she offered, "This is the blood of Christ." It didn't take very long for the congregation of about forty people to line up and commune. About a third of the way down the line stood my son, Aaron. I remember he was grinning from ear to ear as he ambled down the aisle. The whole time his little hands were cupped and extended outward. His eyes were fixed on the bread as he made his way to the front. "This is the body of Christ for you, Aaron," I said to my little cherub, while bending downward and struggling to choke back tears. "Thank you, Daddy!" he replied with a slight giggle. He dipped his bread in the cup. "This is the blood of Christ for you, Aaron," said Sue. After eating the bread, he skipped away. I was trying to refocus my attention on the next person in front of me when I noticed Aaron getting back in line again. He was coming around for seconds! One of his surrogate church grandmothers caught up with him and carried him back to her seat. Aaron sat quietly with her while the last persons communed. After worship Kim and I escorted the family back to the parsonage next door.

As we made our way through the cemetery that separated the little country church from our house, I remember my mother questioning my decision to allow someone so little to commune— even if it was her own grandson. "He has no idea what communion is all about!" she protested. "Well, can you tell me what it means, Mom?" I challenged her. She fumbled through her memory banks to find the "correct" theological answer. As she did, I called Aaron over to us. "Aaron, can you tell Nana what communion means?" Without missing a beat, he lit up and said, "Communion means Jesus loves me." End of story. My mother was reduced to tears. She never again questioned a child's ability to grasp seemingly complex theological things. Worshipers hopefully enter worship as God's little children, with our hands cupped and extended, ready to receive whatever gifts God has for us. Thin space worship intentionally incorporates elements that foster a "God to me" experience. Adults and children gather with the community of faith to receive something from God.

FROM US TO US

As someone who has invested a lifetime in ministry and worship development, I have observed another direction worship seems to have taken in postmodern culture, one that promotes a predominantly *us to us* experience. In some venues people are invited to come and simply be spectators or observers of what others are doing in worship. These seeker-oriented models of worship, like those made popular by Willow Creek (the megachurch near Chicago) and its associated churches, are designed primarily to make unchurched or pre-Christian people—as they are often referred to—feel comfortable in a safe, neutral environment like a theater or concert hall. Little is expected of them. Great care is taken that they not be overly involved in the service. Worship in these venues is performed *for* these seekers *by* well-trained staff. People brand new to the church experience having little or no background in Christianity are invited to come to *watch* others worship God. Willow Creek intentionally designs its Sunday morning worship to reach such seekers. The intent is to meet seekers where they are in worship and then offer a plethora of programs and activities that will meet their needs and connect them with other people. The objective is that these seekers eventually become believers and worship at the church's Wednesday night believers' service.

As the largest program-based, seeker-friendly church in North America, the leadership of Willow Creek has recently confessed that simply meeting people where they are and helping them get plugged into seeker-style worship, programs, and activities that will meet their perceived needs is not necessarily enough to help them grow as Christian disciples. Bill Hybels, senior pastor of Willow Creek Church, recently said, "We made a mistake. What we should have done when people crossed the line of faith and [became] Christians, we should have started telling people and teaching people that they have to take responsibility to become 'self feeders.' We should have gotten people, taught people, how to read their Bible between service[s], how to do the spiritual practices much more aggressively on their own."[2]

In other words, spiritual maturity is less likely to happen when we overemphasize the "us to us" direction in worship and ministry. Willow Creek learned through an extensive qualitative study of its ministry that people mature spiritually through the practices of prayer, Bible reading, and relationships—us to God, God to us, and us to us relationships. A more comprehensive understanding and practice of worship is needed if the church hopes to effectively reach postmodern people for Christ.

An Omnidirectional Approach to Worship

What if church leaders began to think about and plan worship as an omnidirectional, life-transforming experience that happens *within* a faith community where people at varying stages of faith development experience worship as simultaneously us to God, God to us, and us to us? I think an omnidirectional approach would revolutionize the way many churches approach worship. For one thing, it can help us be mindful of the past, present, and future tenses of worship. I am worshiping in the shadow of those saints of the past, the people who are present with me now, all the while anticipating those who will be joining the community of faith today and in the years to come.

My experience at Inch Abbey—as I stood there contemplating its beauty and significance in the spirituality of Northern Ireland—heightened my sense that the saints of ancient times were standing right there with me. But I also find that whenever I worship God, even in a middle-school cafeteria, I can still contemplate the saints of more recent history who likewise lifted their hearts, minds, and voices to the Creator of the Universe. I think of my mother, my in-laws, faithful people who lovingly stewarded the gospel in my life who now worship at the throne of glory. I remember that they are literally with me, separated only by a heartbeat. My voice blends with theirs in praise of God. My hand touches theirs as I receive the bread and cup of communion and when I reach out to take the hand of my neighbor as we bow our heads for the benediction. We are surrounded by such a great cloud of witnesses. Attending to worship as a thin space reminds me of the relational nature of God's kingdom.

Just recently I reminded the congregation that worship isn't something *we* create. We don't turn worship on and off because we begin and end at a prescribed time. Worship isn't something *we* do and invite God into. We intentionally step into the ongoing stream of worship and lend our hearts and voices. Rather than thinking of worship as something we *do* for a limited time or, worse yet, something we *go to* in a specific place, how about if we begin to imagine worship as our participation in an ongoing spiritual drama that has neither a beginning nor an end? Can we get our heads and hearts around the idea that when we give ourselves to worship we join in an already worshiping community that began with God's first creative acts, continues in the present, and extends outward throughout all eternity?

The morning of HopeSpring's first public worship service as a new church, I was awakened at about 4:00 a.m. by what sounded like whispered prayers coming from a multitude of people in a very distant place. As you can imagine, the sensation was a little spooky. As I lay there, desperately wanting to go back to sleep, I couldn't get that sound out of my head. I eventually did drift off to sleep for another hour and didn't give my "dream" another thought. Later in the week, however, I received an e-mail from a Methodist pastor friend in Belfast, Northern Ireland. He wanted to know how our first service went and to tell me that at 9:00 a.m. their time (4:00 a.m. ours), he was leading his congregation in prayer for us. Was it possible I heard their prayers in some supernatural way? I don't know, but why not? Since that dream and e-mail, I am more conscious than ever that whenever our congregation is worshiping God, thousands, perhaps millions, of people near us and around the globe are worshiping God too. When we worship, we step into an activity that is ongoing and all encompassing, involving even the saints of God who have died and surround the heavenly throne. These are people of faith who surround us and encourage us in our journey with God.

A Thin Space That Leans and Kicks

Both intentional connection with the past and innovative push toward the future shape the church's present worship of God. We inherit our faith from those who journeyed before us. We stand in a wonderful succession of those who have passed on what they have known and received from God. The founders of our particular faith "tribes"—such as John and Charles Wesley for the Methodists—and all those who carried their visions forward have acted as spiritual guides for those who continue on the journey. We are now called to be such guides for an emerging faith community. We must lean back into the traditions of our foremothers and forefathers and find innovative ways to carry these traditions forward for coming generations.

Leonard Sweet, nationally acclaimed author and professor, was the person who first told me about parabolic harmonious oscillation, which is a fancy physicist's term for the movement of a swing. Parabolic harmonious oscillation is doing two opposing things at the same time—leaning back and kicking forward. If you live near a swing, try this. Try to move the swing by only leaning back *or* kicking forward. You won't get very far. You must lean *while* you kick. Worship that swings in an imaginative way invites people to lean back—I mean way beyond the 1940s and '50s— into the stories of people who journeyed with God thousands of years ago and shared their accounts in what Christians call the Bible. We lean back into their experiences of God, their wisdom and faithfulness, and the lessons they have provided us. We also lean back into our own faith traditions, incorporating them into our modern worship. Stories, sacraments, liturgies, and symbols remind us where we have been and what we value as a people of God.

LEARNING TO LEAN

Thin spaces may emerge for people in worship partly because worship leaders are willing to work at creating environments that promote an awareness of God's transcendence. This is one of the fundamental tasks of those who plan and lead worship in the church. I have often referred to HopeSpring's worship team as environmentalists. Our careful and prayerful planning of worship must facilitate an environment that will help others connect with God, bond with each other, and open their hands, hearts, and minds to all that God seeks to give them.

In striving to create environments where thin spaces may emerge, we at HopeSpring lean back, regularly incorporating ancient prayer styles such as hesychastic prayer, a contemplative style of prayer widely practiced by the fathers and mothers of the desert in the early days of Christianity. These ordinary men and women of the third and fourth centuries AD sought a life of prayer that often led them away from the distractions of daily life to secluded areas, including deserts, to heighten their experience of God. Hesychastic prayer is believed to have been created by these desert elders. During this prayer, people are invited to sit quietly, with back straight and hands resting in the lap, palms up. We say quietly in our hearts, as we breathe in through our noses, "Lord Jesus, come," or something similar. As we exhale through our mouths we pray, "Take away our fear (anxiety, worry, sin, and so forth)."

We lean back by incorporating another ancient form of prayer known as centering prayer. In this prayer time, people are invited to choose a sacred word as the symbol of their intention to consent to God's presence and action within. Words like surrender, trust, believe, and repent are used to quiet our hearts as we silently abide in God's gracious presence. Whenever our minds begin to wander away from simply being with God, we come back to that word and center ourselves again.

At HopeSpring we also lean back by using Scripture as a means for prayer. The one we use most often is commonly known as *lectio divina* (sacred reading). During this prayer time, a brief scripture passage is read slowly, and people are invited to notice what word or phrase stands out to them. After a period of silence, the reading is repeated as people continue to reflect on that word or phrase. After more silence, the passage is read again. This time people are invited to pray to God about that word or phrase and then express gratitude for the ways God has spoken to them through the scripture.

A decision was made by me early on in HopeSpring's journey as a new church that we would regularly lean back as a sacramental faith community that incorporates communion into each of our worship events. Immediate concerns were raised about the

timing and logistics of doing this every week. But they were quickly countered with statements like, "As a young family we need to
gather around the table as often as possible," and "Since we believe
communion is a means by which God expresses love and grace
to us, why would we *not* want to share in that every week?" We
are presently experimenting with different methods by which we
share and receive this sacrament. Leaning back is something we
strive to practice in each worship service. Because of our heritage
as Christians—and United Methodists—we have a substantial
reservoir of rich traditions into which to lean back.

LEARNING TO KICK

Kicking forward, I believe, means advancing many of the traditions of our faith in a more culturally relevant way. For example,
we at HopeSpring still value retelling the biblical story—it remains
central to our faith—but rather than doing so by reading it aloud
from a pulpit or lectern in an archaic language, like King James
English, we use video, drama, or a storyteller who helps capture
our imagination, drawing us more fully into the story.

Capitalizing on the energy and power from these ancient stories, we kick them forward in innovative ways, using the technology currently available to us, including state-of-the-art audio and
video systems. The people coming to worship with us are inundated throughout the week by high quality multimedia presenta-
tions at work and again at home through high-definition digital
television sets. In 2009 broadcasters will make the switch from
analog to digital signals, relegating most of home television sets
to high-priced doorstops unless people purchase cable or satellite
service or get a converter. I understand that many congregations
find it difficult to compete with the technological excellence we
all take for granted in our everyday lives, and some would argue
that we shouldn't even try. I believe, though, that we need to do
everything we can—with everything we have—to do our very best
to kick the gospel forward in our postmodern world. Here is an
example of what I mean.

Up until now we have discouraged people from using their cell phones during worship. We have placed blurbs in the bulletin asking people to silence these devices. Every now and then someone forgets to set his or hers to "vibrate" and, of course, it goes off right in the middle of my sermon. I have taken to shaming such offenders by offering a quick response like, "I'd like mine with pepperoni and mushrooms. Hold the anchovies!" There is generally some laughter and we move on. There is no place in a sacred worship service for such distractions—or is there? I have recently learned about a way you can incorporate text messaging into worship. A Web-based program I recently discovered allows people in worship to send text messages in real time directly to the screens on the platform in response to a question asked during a sermon, to share prayer requests, or to present the names of departed loved ones during an All Saints' Day service. The program allows you to set limitations on the words people can use in their texts. You can designate a G, PG, or R rating that filters out undesired language. Of course, a certain amount of equipment is required, such as a wireless computer, video projector, and screen. But just imagine the possibilities! What has become a common practice in our culture—text messaging—but is widely considered taboo in worship can now be integrated into the worship experience. We are working toward utilizing this technology at HopeSpring. I think it could be quite powerful to invite people to participate in the ways I mentioned above. I wonder if Jesus had had access to this stuff, would he have found a way to use it too?

Parabolic harmonious oscillation in worship encourages the worship leaders to think creatively about how we can kick the faith forward by using current culture to tell an ancient story that may open us to the awesomeness of God. Kicking the faith forward has less to do with style—traditional, contemporary, blended, or emergent—and more to do with imagination. I think I have participated in almost every conceivable style of worship, and in each of them I have experienced a sense of God's awesome presence—a thin space.

When people try to pin me down about the worship style of HopeSpring, I am intentionally vague. Many people would erroneously describe our worship style as "contemporary." There are contemporary elements, but I don't like that label because in many people's minds the word *contemporary* implies all kick and no lean. We are not "traditional" in the way many people understand that word, because we don't sing out of hymnals or recite many unison prayers and creeds. I am not sure our worship necessarily qualifies as "emerging" either. And I wouldn't describe us as "blended," which I have come to learn—the hard way—means you appeal to no one and offend everyone.

Kicking forward has required that we at HopeSpring learn about the music the unchurched of our area listen to and mirror some of that in our worship songs. This past Sunday our praise band led the congregation in singing an old hymn, "Solid Rock," but with energy and enthusiasm complemented by drums, electric guitar, and keyboard. The congregation—young and old, churched and unchurched—sang it with joy. Kicking forward in worship in an imaginative way means using the cultural tools available today to help people experience thin spaces. The question isn't about how worship connects with culture but how the church uses culture to connect people with God.

Preaching That Leans and Kicks

Preaching in a postmodern culture must also have a lean and kick dynamic. In preaching, preachers *lean* fully back into the Scriptures and traditions of their particular faith tribe and then *kick* the stories of the faith forward through preaching that engages the mind, opens the heart, and fuels the imagination. Preaching that so captivates the mind and heart and evokes a response can help people experience thin spaces.

I recently attended a service at our sponsoring church, St. Luke's, where Beth, one of the associate pastors on staff, preached about justice, using Micah 6:8 as her text. When she concluded her message, she invited us to find a place at one of the prayer stations in the worship space (round tables at the corners of the room). On each table was a specific letter to one of our state representatives voicing concerns about justice issues like poverty and the mistreatment of immigrants in our wider community. By the end of worship that day people had prayed over and signed several hundred letters. The letters were promptly gathered up and mailed the next day. Through her preaching, Beth invited us to lean back into the Scriptures and kick our faith forward to promote a sense of justice in the world.

Before HopeSpring started meeting for its own worship services, I was asked to preach at a more contemporary-style service on All Saints' Day at St. Luke's. Sadly, these liturgical festivals are often ignored in many contemporary-style venues. I planned to use an illustration in my message that referenced stained glass windows. We would be worshiping in a gymnasium, so the worship director and I decided to build a three-sided kiosk with stained glass on each side. We made the window frames out of wood, added Plexiglas panels, and glued odd-shaped translucent patches of colored paper on the inside of each pane. We then wired florescent lights inside the kiosk and placed it in front of the stage.

In my message I spoke about saints as people who allow the light to shine through them. I asked them to think about people who have died who had been light in their lives and to consider inviting God to shine through their own lives. After the message, I invited people to write, on multicolored sticky notes, the name of someone who had been light in their life, then to simply write their own name as an act of committing themselves to God, and then when ready to place the note on the window. After nearly twenty minutes, when the final person placed her note on the window, we turned the lights inside the panels on. It was breathtaking! After the service people gathered around the window to see all the names. Some even took pictures. For the next several weeks, we placed the lighted window, complete with notes, on the stage for worship. Even after two years, people still comment about how meaningful that service was. A thin space emerged in worship that morning in part because the preaching, linked with participation, invited people to both lean back into an ancient celebration of the saints and kick forward, participating in the experience by writing names on sticky notes and stepping forward to place them on the window.

While there is no one formula or right way to design and lead worship, what counts most is worship leaders' desire to create worship environments that allow thin spaces to emerge, helping people lean and kick as they experience transcendence for themselves. Leaders always do this in partnership with God. God takes our heartfelt attempts to create opportunities for thin spaces and elevates them far beyond what we could ever imagine or hope to do alone.

One of the most exciting biblical examples of this is found in 2 Chronicles 5:1–7:11. Notice the omnidirectional experiences in the passage. Solomon has been commissioned by God (God to me) to complete the temple for which his father David planned and provided. The temple is finished. All the furnishings are in place. The Ark, containing only the two stone tablets Moses placed there, is being moved from Zion to Jerusalem.

As it is moved, Solomon and the congregation of Israel (us to us) walk before it, sacrificing more sheep and oxen than could be counted. The Ark is then positioned in its final place in the inner sanctuary of the temple under the wings of the cherubim. Here is where the story gets good. When the priests set the Ark down and step outside the inner sanctuary, the singers, trumpeters, and percussionists (ancient praise band) cut loose (us to God). In unison they sing, "For he is good, for his steadfast love endures forever." The temple is filled with a cloud—the Lord's presence—so much so that the priests, the "lead worshipers," can't continue their work. God became the worship leader that day. In 2 Chronicles 7 the experience is repeated again during the actual dedication of the temple. "When Solomon had ended his prayer, fire came down from heaven and consumed the burnt offering and the sacrifices; and the glory of the LORD filled the temple. The priests could not enter the house of the LORD, because the glory of the LORD filled the LORD's house" (2 Chron. 7:1–2 NRSV). When the people witnessed this grand spectacle, they fell on their faces and worshiped God. Since reading this account many years ago, I have stepped into worship expecting God to so overwhelm me that I wouldn't be able to continue my sermon or that God's presence would so engulf our space that the entire congregation would stand in place with mouths agape!

Thin Spaces Require Our Openness

A few months ago I got to visit Inch Abbey again in the rain—the way it is supposed to be experienced in September. This time I was alone, cold, and wet as I stood next to the place I had previously sat to sketch my picture. Walking around the ruins, I could visualize where I was and what I did during my previous visit. As I circled the ruins I softly spoke a prayer. I thanked God for the wonder of this place, for the opportunity to visit it again so soon, for the thin space I experienced there, and for the abiding sense it gave me that even when I am by myself, I am never really alone. I expressed gratitude for the great cloud of witnesses who made this place sacred by their personal consecration and dedication to a once vibrant religious community.

That beautiful environment, even in the rain, lifted my eyes and heart above the mundane and routine of my life. My openness to the moment heightened my awareness of the spiritual presence of others. I leaned back into the rich history of the abbey and simultaneously found myself kicking forward—thinking about the new church I was called to start. As I walked away from the abbey, I felt as though a part of myself remained there—like a part of me had been assimilated into the thin space. My prayers to God, my sense of awe at the created world around me, my attempts to capture some of its beauty with pencil and paint, the inspiration I found for my own ministry and the appreciation I gained for the people who once lived here seemed to harness some of my own spiritual energy and mingle it with what was already there. What I discovered that day is that when we experience thin spaces in worship, a part of us is assimilated into the expansiveness of God.

My thin space experiences of worship, in Northern Ireland and now in central Florida, have fueled a desire in me to more imaginatively and prayerfully design and implement worship that will assimilate my congregation into the breathtaking reality of God. My prayer for your congregational leadership is that it will be blessed by practices that lean back into the congregation's heritage, embody innovative ways to kick the congregation's story forward for a new generation, all the while desiring to be blown away, as the Israelites were, by a God whose incredible glory fills the house. Lord, let it be!

An Imaginative Exercise

Gather the members of your worship team. In smaller churches, this team may be the pastor and principal musician. In larger congregations, this team might include the worship committee, choir, band members, singers, and so forth. Discuss the following questions:

1. When have you and your team experienced a "thin space" in worship?
2. In what ways is your worship relational: us to God, God to us, and us to us?
3. Using the two simultaneous movements of a swing—leaning and kicking—talk about how you do these things in worship.
4. How is the preaching in your service a lean and a kick event?
5. Based on the discussion you have just had, what in your worship pattern needs to change? What needs to go and what needs to stay? Is there anything you need to add to worship?

CHAPTER 6

❧

Imagining a
Generous Church

I am one of those "glass half full" kind of guys. I tend to see the best in people even when they cannot see it in themselves, which gets me into trouble sometimes and almost always keeps me from serving on juries.

As a "glass half full" theologian and pastor, I have always emphasized the notion of original goodness over original sin. While I can't discount the theological construct of the fall—I find way too much empirical evidence around *and* within me to discredit that—I have chosen to put more emphasis in my preaching and teaching on the notion of original goodness. After putting the final brushstroke on the cosmic canvas of creativity God stepped back, with squinted eyes surveyed the finished work, and said, "Wow! That's good. That's *really* good." You and I were in the center of that work. We still are! The Scriptures remind us that when God looks at us, he sees the reflection of himself: "So God created human beings in his own image. In the image of God he created them; male and female he created them" (Gen. 1:27 NLT). What greater compliment can we be given than that?

Being created in the image of God has nothing to do with our physical attributes and everything to do with our qualities and characteristics. Among all the things I know God to be (creative, transforming, liberating, and just) I believe that God is—at the very core—generous. And because you and I are made in the image of God, we too are by nature generous. To be generous means to be "liberal in giving or sharing. Open-handed."[1] When I imagine what the church can be in all its fullness, I envision a community of faith that is, at its very core, generous—giving, sharing, and openhanded.

Lots of people would argue that U.S. citizens, and particularly U.S. Christians, are stingy and self-indulgent. I have seen some of the statistics used to support this argument. It doesn't change my belief that generosity is as much a part of human nature as love, faith, and hope. Whether we can learn to express this generosity in outward, God-honoring ways is the question. Just as love has its opposite, indifference; and faith has its opposite, fear; and hope has its opposite, despair; generosity also has its opposite, greed. When we lack a divine center, these negative attributes lead us into a spiritual amnesia. We forget who and whose we are. Richard Foster refers to this as a psychosis, because when indifference, fear, despair, and greed characterize our lives, we have lost complete touch with reality—the reality that we are, by God's design, generous. Foster writes: "This psychosis permeates even our mythology. The modern hero is the poor boy who becomes rich rather than the Franciscan or Buddhist ideal of a rich boy who voluntarily becomes poor. (We still find it hard to imagine that either could happen to a girl!) Covetousness we call ambition. Hoarding we call prudence. Greed we call industry."[2]

As leaders in the church we must first recognize this psychosis in ourselves, work to recover what is God's design for us, and then through words and action lead people to rediscover their generous selves in Christ.

Generosity has become somewhat en vogue these days, thanks to high profile philanthropists, such as Bill and Melinda Gates, Bono, Ted Turner, and Warren Buffet, who are giving away substantial portions of their wealth to help eliminate global poverty, AIDS, malaria, and infectious diseases. Because of their fame, we are captivated by their generosity. And while their giving is truly inspiring, I can't help but wonder if it is just a passing fad—the latest trend among the trendy, although I hope not. The glass-half-full part of me would like to think that, through them, other people in our culture will become more generous too.

The church has historically helped channel people's generosity, as has been evidenced most recently in response to the natural disasters in the United States and in Asia. An article published in *USA Today* reports that U.S. citizens gave away nearly $300 billion to charitable causes in 2006, breaking a previous record set in 2005 by a generous outpouring of aid to the victims of Hurricanes Katrina, Rita, and Wilma and the Asian tsunami. The biggest chunk of the donations, $96.82 billion or 32.8 percent, went to religious organizations. About 65 percent of households with incomes less than $100,000 give to a charity of some kind.[3] As I am writing this chapter, Myanmar has been devastated by a cyclone that may have taken nearly one hundred thousand lives. The outpouring of assistance from around the world already is heartwarming. It is predicted that personal charitable donations to aid in the recovery of Burma may exceed any previously set records.

People are by nature generous, but we can be somewhat confused in the way we exercise generosity. As admirable as our giving has been toward others who have experienced hardship and pain, it is often eclipsed by our propensity to spend billions of dollars every year on frivolous things. I researched U.S. citizens' spending and found that:

- Halloween candy sales in 2005 were up for the third year in a row to an estimated $2.1 billion; the growth was 2.3 percent on top of growth of 2.4 percent the previous year.[4]
- In 2003, Americans spent an average of $835 on holiday gifts.[5]
- Analysts at Goldman Sachs estimate that the global beauty industry—consisting of skin-care products worth $24 billion; makeup, $18 billion; $38 billion of hair-care products; and $15 billion of perfumes—is growing at up to 7 percent a year, more than twice the rate of the developed world's GDP (gross domestic product).[6]

- Americans spend over $9 billion annually on dog food.[7]
- Gambling has become a booming industry in the United States. From 1974 to 1994—twenty years—the amount of money people in the United States legally wagered rose 2,800 percent, from $17 billion to $482 billion.[8]
- Americans now spend more money on fast food than they do on higher education, personal computers, software, or new cars. They spend more on fast food than on movies, books, magazines, newspapers, videos, and recorded music—combined.[9]

Imagine the good and wholesome things that could have been accomplished with all those resources. According to Jim Sheppard, chief executive officer and principal of Generis Partners—a company that provides stewardship and fund-raising counsel to churches and nonprofit organizations:

> The last 50 years in the United States has produced an unprecedented outbreak of affluence. In the face of this condition, Americans—especially Christian Americans—have struggled to understand how to manage financial resources in a way that is consistent with their faith. Without clear teaching and instruction, church members have absorbed more of what the world says than what the Bible says about money and possessions. Christians have brought this thinking back into the void that existed in their local congregations, creating a damaging impact on the Biblical understanding of money and possessions.[10]

According to Sheppard, church leaders face a serious challenge in our churches. How do we encourage and invite people to be the generous people God created them to be in the face of all the distractions competing for their attention and affections? Advocating such generosity takes bold and courageous leaders. It also requires the church, as community, to understand and embrace the mind and heart of God in this matter.

Generosity Flows When the Dam of Fear Is Broken

In my work as a stewardship consultant I have been privileged to come alongside churches that dreamed great dreams and saw grand visions of what God intended them to be. I helped these churches understand that the key to making their dreams become reality was how well their leaders could teach and model generosity among their people. Through an intentional four- to six-month process, I would coach the leaders to effectively communicate their vision, involve a large percentage of the congregation in some form of meaningful activity related to the process, teach biblical stewardship principles, and invite people into prayer and discernment about their generous financial response. In the beginning stages of nearly every one of these adventures, the leaders of the church expressed fear and doubt. They were *afraid* to ask people to be generous because they *doubted* the people had the desire or the means to do so.

In an article in the Alban Institute's *Congregations* magazine, "The Art of the Ask: Getting Good at Fundraising," pastor and author Donna Schaper writes, "Many clergy don't ask people for money simply because they are so afraid of suffering the embarrassment of being told 'no' that they just keep saying, 'I'll do anything for you, Jesus, but please don't make me ask anyone for money.'"[11]

I understand this fear and doubt. I have been there myself. But I have come to learn that one of my most important tasks as a spiritual leader and guide is learning how to invite people to exercise their generosity in God-honoring ways by helping them discover and maintain a posture of openness that allows the gifts of God to flow freely in *and through* their lives and back out again into the world. Such generosity comes only as people begin to trust the provisions of God for their lives.

In his best-selling book, *Celebration of Discipline*, author Richard Foster writes: "We cling to our possessions rather than sharing them because we are anxious about tomorrow. But if we truly believe that God is who Jesus said He is, then we do not need to be afraid. When we come to see God as the almighty Creator *and* our loving Father we can share because we know that he will care for us."[12] Selfishness or greed stems from a lack of trust in God. The hands of the untrusting and fearful tighten their grip around the gifts God has given and are reluctant to release them for the good of others.

I remember watching a documentary on monkeys in Africa and how attracted they are not only to food but also to shiny things. Once they get their hands around something they want, it is nearly impossible to get them to let it go. The narrator illustrated how monkeys easily get caught as a result of their greediness. Boxes are constructed with a hole in the top just large enough for a monkey's hand to pass through. An object is placed inside the box so that, when the money grasps it, the monkey's hand becomes too large to extract from the box. Even though it may be in danger of getting captured or killed, the monkey refuses to let go.

Though this drama seems comical on one hand, it is quite unnerving on the other, especially when I consider how much I am like that monkey. When I find something I want or *think* I need, I am reluctant to open my hand and allow that thing to pass from my fingers along a pathway God intends. But generosity requires just such openness.

Jesus was aware of how important generosity is for us, and that is why he spoke about possessions more than any other subject—as recorded by the Gospel writers. For example, sixteen of the thirty-eight parables Jesus taught dealt with money or possessions. One in ten Gospel verses is about money or possessions. While there are about five hundred verses in the Bible about prayer and fewer than five hundred about faith, there are more than two thousand verses about money and possessions!

Jesus summed it all up when he said, "For where your treasure is, there your heart will be also" (Luke 12:34 NRSV).

"Affluenza" Is the Enemy of Generosity

To be a fruitful church in the twenty-first century I believe will require radical generosity from each of us in the church, which will in turn compel us to wage war against the disease of "affluenza" in our own lives and culture. Affluenza is the enemy of generosity. The English word *affluence* comes from the Latin *affluentem*, which means "flowing freely."[13]

I have a vivid picture of affluenza in my mind that goes back nearly thirty years to a month I spent in Israel studying history, geography, and archaeology. With forty other students from around the world, I got to experience the Holy Land without all the hype and commercialism typical of most organized church tours. I got to participate in an archaeological dig; spent many evening meals with a Palestinian Arab family whom I had befriended; and crisscrossed most of the country on foot, following the goat and sheep paths that snaked through the dry, chalky wilderness and stopping at the occasional oasis that seemed to appear out of nowhere. Our group visited some of the more common touristy sites, such as the Church of the Holy Sepulchre (one of the three places in Jerusalem Jesus is said to have risen from the dead), Skull Hill (one of two places where it is purported that Jesus was crucified), the Mount of Transfiguration, and natural sites like the Jordan River, the Sea of Galilee, and the Dead Sea.

The Dead Sea is not very generous. I had heard that the Dead Sea had an unusual smell but I wasn't prepared for just how stinky it really is. Most people manage to ignore the stench long enough to wade into the sea and float effortlessly on the mineral rich water. I wimped out and kept my distance—upwind. From its northern boundary, the Dead Sea receives a steady influx of fresh, clean water from the Sea of Galilee channeled by the Jordan River. The Dead Sea takes it all in *and* keeps it to itself! Because there are no natural outlets from the Dead Sea, the fresh clean water that flows into it soon becomes stagnant and relatively lifeless. Such is the fate of those stricken with the spiritual disease of affluenza.

Jesus declared war on affluenza when he saw the lack of generosity even modest wealth can breed in people. He condemned materialism as a rival to God: "No slave can serve two masters; for a slave will either hate the one and love the other, or be devoted to the one and despise the other. You cannot serve God and wealth" (Luke 16:13 NRSV). Jesus knew the grip that affluence can have on a person, which is why he instructed those who would follow after him, "Do not store up for yourselves treasures on earth, where moth and rust consume and where thieves break in and steal" (Matt. 6:19 NRSV). Advocating a lifestyle of generosity, Jesus said, "Give to everyone who begs from you; and if anyone takes away your goods, do not ask for them again" (Luke 6:30 NRSV). By comparison, Jesus lived in a much simpler society than ours. If he was *that* concerned about the dangers of affluence for people then, imagine how much more concerned he must be for people like us who live in such a highly affluent culture.

Affluenza suggests that whatever flows into our lives never goes back out again. In one of my favorite devotional books, *The Music of Silence: Entering the Sacred Space of Monastic Experience*, author David Steindl-Rast, OSB, suggests that our lives are like a barrel, and affluence demands that when our barrels are full and the excess is ready to spill over onto others in beautiful and beneficial ways, we make our barrels bigger so that they can accommodate more.

The economics of affluence demand that things that were special for us last year must now be taken for granted; so the container gets bigger, and the joy of overflowing gratefulness is taken away from us. But if we make the vessel smaller and smaller by reducing our needs, then the overflowing comes sooner and with it the joy of gratefulness. It is the overflow that sparkles in the sun.[14]

Generosity intentionally has us constraining the size of our barrels so that we keep only what we need and, when more blessings flow our way, allow them to spill out in blessing to others. I know people who have purposely waged war on affluenza in their lives and are filled with the joy of gratefulness of which Steindl-Rast writes. Close friends of ours have learned to cap their standard of living so that as they earn more money, they have more to

give away. Kim and I have been the recipients of their generosity—
and many others have been, too. Though our financial resources
are drastically different from theirs, Kim and I also strive to con-
strain the size of our barrel so that we too may become more generous with others.

Inspired by the Generosity of Others

In one of the stewardship campaigns I directed for a church in
Iowa, the pastor and I were confronted by an older woman who
made it clear to us that she lived on a fixed income and had no
plans to give any more money to her church. I thanked her for her
honesty and said something like, "Your church isn't asking you
for money right now but for prayer. Please pray and seek to know
God's will for you in this." She replied that she was one of the
prayer warriors of the church; so, the pastor invited her to organize two or three other prayer warriors she knew and get together regularly with them to lift up the vision and direction of the
church. She readily accepted the invitation and by the next morning called the pastor to tell him the names of the other people on
her prayer team. I didn't have any other contact with this woman
until the very end of my consultation with the congregation. She
caught me outside the sanctuary doors one Sunday morning and
handed me a piece of paper. I have kept it these past ten years because it has been such a powerful testimony of generosity for me.
Handwritten on the note was a makeshift spreadsheet under the
heading, "My Gift to Rise Up and Build" (which was the name of
the church's campaign). Here is what it said:

Cash from the interest on my investments	$10,000
My birthday lunches out the next three years	$300
Clothing I won't buy (I already have enough)	$250
Crafts I will make and sell	$2,000
Cookies I won't eat	$30
Total	$12,580

As I recall, the church exceeded its goal by a little more than $10,000. The generosity of this woman living on a fixed income pushed them over the top!

The same year I worked with the church in Iowa, I consulted a small church in Kentucky. Every time the church had a meeting related to its stewardship program, a middle-aged man would come and ask to speak to the people gathered. Each time he spoke his message was essentially the same: "I am against making any changes to our building and asking people to give more money than they're already giving to the church." The pastor would let the man speak his mind and then continue the meeting. This happened at least a dozen times over three months. There would be an audible groan from people whenever he walked into the room. Each time, the pastor or I would encourage people to keep an open mind and prayerfully discern how God wanted them to be involved in the process. By the end of the process, the man had succeeded to persuade a few other influential families to join his protest.

The Sunday the pastor planned to invite people to offer their commitments to the church's vision, the man stood up again, before the pastor could speak, and asked if he could say a few words. The pastor looked at me, sitting near the front, for some direction. I shrugged my shoulders as if to say, "I guess you're going to have to let him speak his mind—*again*." I held my breath as the man ambled down the aisle to the platform. "Please be brief," I heard the pastor whisper to him as he held his hand over the microphone. The man took a deep breath and began. I recall the essence of his remarks this way:

> You all know that I have been dead set against this thing from the very beginning. I've heard everyone talking about God's vision for our church and our need to make some changes around here. There's been lots of talk about asking God to work through us to accomplish his will for the church. And we've been asked to pray before we decide what God wants us to do. About three weeks ago I started doing just that—praying for God to show

me his will. At first I thought I could give a couple hundred dollars and just be done with it. But that's not what God wanted from me. I thought about some other ways I could give more. But what I thought I heard God saying he wanted from me was more than just a token gift. He wanted me to give something that had real value to me.

At this point the man started to choke up. He reached into his pocket and pulled out a set of keys. Everyone else gasped. They understood what the keys represented. So did the pastor, who also started to cry. The man held out the keys to an antique truck he had restored from the frame up—at a great cost of time and money. "Pastor," he continued, "you better take these keys from me. I don't know how long I'm going to be able to dangle them out there." The pastor snatched the keys to the man's prized possession and embraced him. The congregation erupted in applause. It was a beautiful thing to experience. Generosity always is. Some of the people influenced early on by this man's dissention were moved by his change of heart and offered their own gifts to the church.

In another church the children's department created colorful coin banks out of shoeboxes. Each box was divided into three labeled compartments: "Tithing 10%," "Saving 10%," "Spending 80%." The children were encouraged to put whatever money they received from gifts, chores, and so on into each of the compartments. The church found a clever way to teach the 10-10-80 principle of money management—a tithe to God, a tithe for savings, and the rest for living expenses. Most adults haven't learned this simple financial plan. Teaching generosity to our children may help raise up more generous adults.

In Richmond, Virginia, two siblings named Kyle, age four, and Lydia, age five, placed a heavy paper bag on the altar of their church during the Sunday morning offering time. Everyone was curious about the contents of the bag. Immediately following worship the treasurer opened the bag to retrieve a note folded neatly on top of a pile of coins. The note read, "Here is our gift to God, because we love the Lord and our church. This is a whole bag of pennies. We can only count to twenty, so we don't know how much is in here, but it is a lot! Thank you for using our pennies to serve Jesus."

Over the years I have collected dozens of stories like these that I like to share as examples of generosity and to encourage faithful giving to God's work. Unfortunately, not every story I know has a happy ending. Affluenza can keep some people from being the generous folks God created them to be.

What's Mine Is Mine and What's Yours Is Mine

I remember walking through the home of a fairly wealthy family who took great pride in the antiques they had collected from around the world. All of the furniture in their home was well over fifty years old. Many of the pieces dated back to colonial times. As they guided me through their personal museum, they delighted in telling me stories of how they found each piece, how extremely rare it was, and what it cost them. As I followed them through the house, it suddenly struck me that everything sitting in their home had at one time sat in someone else's home and that when these folks died, it was all to be redistributed again to other places. We truly don't own a thing in this world. When it came time to make a pledge to their church, they wrote on their card, "Cannot give at this time." They decided to "invest" their money in more furniture.

The weirdest experience I ever had as a stewardship consultant came when a prominent family in a church invited the pastor and me to visit them one evening for coffee and dessert. The pastor had identified this family as having potential to make a major commitment to the church's relocation project. We sipped coffee in their modest home and chitchatted for some time before the husband invited us to follow him down a flight of stairs that began on the inside of their kitchen pantry. The stairs ended abruptly at what appeared to be a heavy bank-vault door. It had one of those spinning wheels you turn after you have successfully navigated the combination. In seconds the man managed to set the combination and spin the wheel. He grunted as he pulled the heavy door toward us. Once inside he flipped a series of switches that illuminated a two-thousand-square-foot warehouse of collectibles placed neatly on racks or inside the kind of glass cases you find in a jewelry store. There were guns, swords, steak knives, lanterns, letter openers, combs, and other objects, all produced by Colt. I knew Colt made handguns but had no idea how diversified they were until the man spent the next hour regaling us with the story behind each treasure he had discovered in the trips he had made around the world. Apparently, Colt collectibles are *big* business. I remember he showed us steak knives that were prototypes of a set that never went into production. He had the one and only set ever made. The six knives were worth $250,000! I found myself getting excited on behalf of the pastor. One carefully chosen item from this room could purchase the land needed for the church's relocation. After their stewardship campaign had ended, I got a call from the pastor. He was heartbroken. While many struggling families gave sacrificially to the vision of their church, the "Colt" family committed $500. According to the note on their card, giving more just wasn't in their budget.

Generosity as a Sign of Kingdom Living

We are tempted at times to think of generosity as an event—an offering we place in a plate, a dollar we hand to a homeless person, a commitment we make to a building program. But Jesus calls us to embrace generosity as a lifestyle.

For Jesus, generosity is one of the defining characteristics of those who belong to the kingdom of God. In Matthew 6 we find Jesus's teaching about trusting God and not worrying about the material things we need to live. Jesus said, "Indeed your heavenly Father knows that you need all these things." And then he added, "But strive first for the kingdom of God and his righteousness, and all these things will be given to you as well" (vv. 32–33 NRSV).

Lifestyle generosity comes only when we seek the kingdom of God and his righteousness *before all else*. As we do that, everything we *need* (not necessarily want) will come in its proper time.

Of this kingdom mind-set that Jesus espoused, Richard Foster writes: "We work but we know that it is not our work that gives us what we have. We live by grace even when it comes to 'daily bread.' We are dependent upon God for the simplest elements of life: air, water, sun. What we have is not the result of our labor, but of the gracious care of God."[15] When we understand this, our hands and hearts naturally open to allow the gifts of God to flow *in* and *through* us and we are less likely to hoard them for ourselves.

One of the greatest challenges my denomination, and probably yours, faces in this century is the rising cost of doing ministry and the stagnant or declining giving of people to the church. Churches like mine have to provide support for clergy that often includes an established minimum salary, housing, health care, pension, and other expenses. In smaller to midsized churches, the pastor's compensation alone can account for nearly fifty percent, or more, of the church's budget. Add to this the skyrocketing costs for insuring facilities, increasing costs for staff health care, and utilities, and many churches find themselves facing financial disaster. Larger churches are by no means impervious to this. I have heard the senior pastor of St. Luke's United Methodist Church, Orlando, Florida, say to other pastors who envy megachurches like St. Luke's because of the size of its budget, "We have the same problems you do. It's just a matter of zeros. Whatever it is you struggle with, add a couple zeros to it, and that's where we are."

For several months now St. Luke's staff has worked hard to hold the line on any budget increases over last year. The national economic challenges of 2008 have hit central Florida really hard because so much of its economy is based on the entertainment and theme-park industry. When disposable income shrinks in most households, a trip to Florida's theme parks usually gets postponed or cancelled altogether. Limiting spending, as a church staff, is a good first step but only a first step. We need to encourage generosity. We know the reality is that if more of our members exercised generosity as faithful stewards, we would have more money flowing into our coffers than we would know what to do with. But how do we get our members to live more generously? Jim Sheppard of Generis Partners says: "Members are acting and thinking more like consumers (eager spenders) than stewards (faithful managers). From 1968 to 1994, discretionary income increased by 54% after taxes and inflation were factored out. During that same period, charitable giving as a percentage of income declined 21% (from 2.5% to about 2%)."[16]

While there are no easy fixes, there are certainly steps we can and should take to become a more generous church.

A Call to Congregational Generosity

First of all, the church—corporately—has to become a much better steward or manager of God's resources. Wise churches are holding their activities up against the light of their vision and values and deciding what needs to continue, and should be supported financially, and what needs to simply stop. Even programs that may not be supported by the budget often drain away staff resources that diminish the energy needed to do what is mission essential. Is it possible that one of the reasons people give such a small percentage of their finances (and perhaps their time) to the church is because they are not sure it is such a good investment?

For churches to become better role models of generosity means they have to be much more careful about the way they invest the resources people entrust to them. Too many churches have never met a program idea they didn't like. If something sounds good or has met with success in other congregations, churches can be too quick to add it to their already full plate of ministries. Given the financial struggles most churches are experiencing these days, I think this means the church has to intentionally engage in an activity or program diet and prioritize the allocation of its resources.

Rather than creating programs and events that compete against each other for people's time and financial resources, it makes better stewardship sense to discern what the most important things are that the church wants people to experience together in the community of faith. Narrowing the scope of ministries prevents us from lapsing into a smorgasbord style of church that can spread our resources way too thin and detract from the main course—who we are and what we are called by God to be. Focus is one of the keys of healthy stewardship.

When we imagine a church that not only sees—but extends—hope in a world of change, it means we form more intentional strategic partnerships with other community-based organizations. HopeSpring considered starting a food pantry to serve people of our larger community. We looked around for space in our building to warehouse the food donations we would receive. We discussed which staff person could oversee the enlistment and training of volunteers to run the food pantry. We considered things like hours of operation, security on site, and how and when we would collect the food. Someone mentioned to me a church that was already operating a food bank closer to the city of Orlando. Through its grocery-store-type mission, this food bank was already serving nearly seven thousand people every month. A couple leaders from our church met with their part-time director and learned that they were desperate for volunteers to come and simply clean and stock shelves. Our church now has a partnership with this organization. The fourth Saturday of every month, members of our congregation are invited to drop in and spend an hour or two helping another congregation do what would be extremely difficult and expensive for us to do.

Most of the public schools in our area struggle to find enough staff and other resources to adequately support their arts programs. Rather than creating, and staffing, arts programs in churches to meet this need, wouldn't it make more sense to partner with schools by sending volunteers to staff *their* programs? Generous churches find more effective ways to become better partners with the communities they are called by God to serve.

Leaders Must Go First

Healthy stewardship in the local church has to begin with the leaders of the congregation. Leaders have to go first. The number of lay leaders I have met who tell me how little their pastors give financially to the church continually shocks me. I am not bragging when I say that Kim and I have always strived to tithe to ministry and mission. Over nearly thirty years together, there may have been a year or two when we gave less than ten percent of our income back to God through the church. As the pastoral leader of a congregation, however, I feel it is my responsibility to model generosity. If I am not doing that, how on earth could I with integrity encourage others to do so? In my preaching, on occasion, I share what Kim and I give to the church. I want people to know the financial amount and that it represents a tithe. I want them to know that practicing generosity is part of what it means to follow Christ. I want them to know that we are willing to go first.

In 1 Chronicles 29, God has given Solomon the task of building the temple. David, his father, lends his support by helping raise the necessary funds. As *the* appointed leader of Israel, David announces what he has given out of his own personal resources to the cause—112 *tons* of gold and more than 262 *tons* of refined silver. He shares this amount openly with his faith community and then challenges them, "Who then will offer willingly, consecrating themselves today to the LORD?" (v. 5 NRSV). Look what happens next. "Then the *leaders* of ancestral houses made their freewill offerings, as did also the leaders of the tribes, the commanders of the thousands of the hundreds, and the officers over the king's work" (v. 6 NRSV, emphasis added). The leaders go first. Their generosity becomes infectious. "Then the people rejoiced because these [*leaders*] had given willingly, for with single mind they had offered freely to the LORD; King David also rejoiced greatly" (v. 9 NRSV). Doesn't that give you goose bumps? When leaders lead with generosity, their giving becomes contagious. Modeling generosity can inspire the church to do great things for God and the world.

Leaders Must Provide Clear Direction

My father often repeated the maxim, "Actions speak louder than words." I believe that's true; however, we would do well to support our actions *with* our words. Leaders in the church, lay and clergy alike, must speak on behalf of generosity. At a recent St. Luke's council meeting, we were deliberating over our budget, spinning ideas around of how we might cut costs. One of the newer leaders listened quietly for a while and then spoke up: "Cutting back on the things we're doing that do not support God's vision for us is always a good idea. But that isn't enough. We have to find ways to increase giving. Everyone of us around this table should go home and think and pray about how we can increase our giving to the church. Maybe there are some things in our lifestyles that shouldn't be as important as they are. If we give some of them up we could do more to advance the kingdom." His words stopped us in our tracks. If one of the pastors around the table had said exactly the same thing, the impact would have been much different—weaker. When lay leaders in the church speak up for generosity, and challenge their peers to give more, the impact is powerful.

One of the important tasks of clergy is to clearly and passionately communicate the vision of the church, through preaching and teaching, and to invite people to support that vision. Asking people to pledge to the budget is never a good idea. Budgets are lifeless tools, a way to target spending and monitor progress. Asking people to generously support vision invites them to enter into the supernatural realm of God's activity.

It occasionally becomes necessary for the pastor, and perhaps some selected lay leaders, to invite specific people to be extraordinarily generous. Every church I have ever served had one or more members who had significant financial means. God has blessed some folks with more resources than others *and* wants them to use those resources for his work. It becomes the responsibility of leadership to invite such folks to give out of their abundance. I am not sure why, but most of these well-off folks wait to be asked before they offer their resources.

I remember coaching a pastor in central Pennsylvania who decided to visit one of the congregation's wealthier members to ask him for $500,000. He knew the man could write that kind of a check but was concerned about how best to approach him. I walked him through a simple process, but as he got closer to his appointment, he got cold feet. He wanted me to go with him for moral support. We made the short jaunt to the man's home and were welcomed warmly by him and his wife. Though extremely nervous, my pastor friend stuck with his plan. He thanked the couple for seeing him and spent about ten minutes painting a picture of his vision for their church. He talked about the resources it would take to make that vision become reality. Then, looking the man right in the eye, said, "I know you are a man of some financial means and that you are one of the most generous givers in the church. I need you to dig more deeply into the resources God has given you and give your church $500,000 to help fund this vision." There was an awkward silence. I cautioned the pastor ahead of time not to break such silence, should it happen. We sat there watching the man exchange glances with his wife. There was no sign of emotion on their faces. After several minutes the man leaned forward toward the pastor and said, "We knew you were coming to ask us for money. We had already talked and prayed together about what we might do for our church. A half a million dollars was the amount we had already planned on." The couple probably would have given their gift to the church without the pastor asking for it, but you never know. The joy it brought my friend, who had garnered the courage to ask, was enormous and well worth the visit. We cannot allow our fear of asking for commitment to rob people of the blessings that come from partnering with God.

Generosity Always Costs Us Something

To generously support God's work, we often have to make some difficult adjustments to the way we spend our resources—personally and corporately as the church. Time has become a precious commodity. For people to serve the church in positions of leadership or in areas of ministry means they have to say no to other things. For people to offer generous financial gifts to the church means they often have to change their spending patterns, make due with an older car, live in a smaller home, forgo a vacation, or something equally sacrificial. One of the definitions I have used for sacrifice is, "Doing away with or setting aside something I value for the sake of something I value more." I witnessed this kind of sacrificial generosity in a doctor in Kentucky. When the lease was up on his Lincoln Town Car, he traded it in on a four-cylinder Chevy Cavalier, saving about $450 a month in payments, which he generously added to his gifts to the church. As a bonus, whenever his colleagues asked about his new wheels, he told them about how the money he was saving was helping his church establish a new ministry in their community. Generosity costs us something and in return gives us the joy of knowing we are working for things that are eternal.

When King David found the land God wanted him to secure for building the temple, he met with the owner, Ornan the Jebusite, to buy it from him. David said to Ornan, "Give me the site of the threshing floor that I may build on it an altar to the LORD—give it to me at its full price." Ornan, recognizing David, offered it to the king without price. He decided to throw in his oxen for burnt offerings, his wood for the fire, and his wheat for a grain offering. "I give it all," he said. How generous! Look at David's response to Ornan: "No; I will buy them for the full price. I will not take for the LORD what is yours, nor offer burnt offerings that cost me nothing" (1 Chron. 21:22–24 NRSV). David's gift to God needed to cost him something personally. Generosity needs to cost us something too.

I truly am one of those glass-half-full kind of guys. I want to see the best in others—even when they can't seem to see it in themselves—and invite them to be the generous people God created them to be. As I contemplate my ongoing leadership role in the church, I want to encourage other leaders to experience generosity for themselves *and* become excited about inviting others to do so.

So let's make our barrels smaller by reducing our own need for more stuff. Let's allow the blessings of God to fill us to overflowing so that those blessings may soak the people around us. The overflow from our generosity sparkles in the sun and brings joy to the God who created us.

Reflection Questions

1. How have you experienced the generosity of God? Of others?
2. How is generosity taught and encouraged in your congregation?
3. How does "affluenza" influence your life? Your congregation?
4. What would it take for you personally (and for your church corporately) to purposely limit the size of your barrels?
5. Discuss this quote from Richard Foster: "What we have is not the result of our labor, but of the gracious care of God."[17]
6. How does your church model generosity? Do the people of your church consider your leaders to be good stewards of the gifts they offer? Why or why not?
7. Generosity always costs us something. What does it cost you? Your church?

CHAPTER 7

❧

Imagining Church as a Life-Saving Station

*I*n our thirty-plus years of ministry together, Gary and I have never found any community quite like the local congregation. We have heard Bill Hybels say on more than one occasion, "The church is the hope of the world!" As the corporate incarnation of Christ, the church has always been a central part of God meeting the world, interacting with it, and offering transformation. This is why we remain committed to it, even after thirty-plus years of our own bumps and bruises, and spend even more time imagining how the church can better offer hope in a world of change.

We have found that one of the blessings, and at times curses, of being in ministry is that we can never fully turn it off. We have taken vacations and respites with the full intention of disengaging our minds from the church only to catch ourselves talking about it, griping about it, and even imagining new possibilities for it. Because we have never been good at leaving it totally behind, we have agreed that while we don't *intend* to make everything in our lives about "church," we *will* embrace the serendipitous insights and ideas that come to us unsolicited, even when we are trying our best to get away from it. I remember one such occasion when we were vacationing with our sons at a place as far away from our

church as we could travel by car. As you will see, it even managed
to follow us there.

Chincoteague Island in Virginia is the Shockley family's favorite vacation spot. This island is a small fishing village where Mar-
guerite Henry made the wild pony Misty famous in her book *Misty
of Chincoteague*. The best thing for us about this vacation spot is
the wealth of activities we have found available to entertain our
family as we grew up over the years. Aaron was three months old
on his first visit and happily surveyed the beach from the backpack
in which he rode while his dad provided transportation. Over the
years we have hiked, enjoyed the ocean, boogey boarded, kayaked,
bicycled (even with training wheels), toured the lighthouse and
several maritime museums, visited the NASA Space Center visitors area, and eaten every imaginable type of seafood, including
the blue crabs that we caught from the pier using chicken necks
and string.

Assateague Island National Seashore is a national wildlife
refuge, and it is the only way to enjoy the ocean when you visit
Chincoteague. As a barrier island and a refuge, Assateague Island
is uninhabited except for a wealth of wild ponies, sika deer, and
thousands of species of birds. We have explored many parts of
this island by bicycle and have found it to be one of God's most
precious gifts. It is a protected area managed by the National Park
Service, which provides interesting programs and displays that
capture the history of both Assateague and Chincoteague Islands.
The last time we visited, the boys were teens, and we decided to
impose a park ranger session upon them and signed up for a
nighttime ghost tour of the beach. What a great experience for
all of us! The boys were enthralled with the ghost crabs crawling
all around us and the ghost stories the rangers told, while Gary
and I had our first lesson on the United States Life-Saving Service
(USLSS), a turn-of-the-century, government-sponsored, ocean-
rescue organization. As we listened to the rangers' stories about
this group, we immediately thought of the church.

A Vision for the Church

As we stood on the beach that night, the Assateague park rangers told the story of a USLSS station once located on that beach at the turn of the nineteenth century. The primary task of the men serving in the USLSS station was to be on the lookout for ships in trouble off the barrier island and provide whatever assistance they could to bring sailors and passengers to safety. On this particular breezy July evening, the men's duties didn't seem like too treacherous an adventure, but we have also visited this beach when it was cold and rainy, and we have been there shortly after hurricanes have whipped through the area, destroying the dunes and flooding the islands, so we knew that danger to ships did exist.

The USLSS began its work as early as 1785 along the Massachusetts shoreline. In the beginning simple huts were built and stocked with food, kindling, and fuel for anyone shipwrecked who managed to somehow make it to shore. While these survival huts offered some help to those in peril, they weren't enough for those in real danger in the sea. In 1803 those who were working these first life-saving stations began using lifeboats—outfitted from whaleboats—to aid in their ocean rescues. In 1807 the first lifeboat station was introduced into the USLSS at Cohasset, Massachusetts, southeast of Boston.

These first stations were staffed primarily by volunteers, and without adequate funding and supervision quickly fell into disrepair. Many of them were vandalized by thieves. It wasn't until the catastrophic winter of 1870–71, with well-publicized shipwrecks occurring all along the Atlantic coast and the Great Lakes, that the United States Congress appropriated $200,000 to create a more effective life-saving system. The Secretary of the Treasury was given the task of employing crews of surfmen and stationing them along the areas of greatest need.[1]

By 1914 the USLSS was organized into thirteen districts along the Atlantic, Pacific, and Great Lake coasts. There were 271 staffed life-saving stations and 8 houses of refuge (along the coast of

Florida).[2] The staff of each station was led by a keeper who lived at the station, usually with his family. Typically six to eight surfmen were assigned to each station. In Florida, the houses of refuge were staffed mainly by one keeper with one boat who provided the necessary food, clothing, and supplies to those who made it ashore from shipwrecks. Evidently, if you want to be in a shipwreck, the Atlantic coast of Florida is the least dangerous place to do so!

When the USLSS transitioned from a mostly volunteer organization to a well-funded and well-managed system, there was an "astounding 87.5% decrease in shipwreck deaths within the areas covered by the Life-Saving Service."[3] Further improvements and organizational efforts paved the way for the USLSS to transition, in 1915, into what we now know as the United States Coast Guard. By the end of the forty-three years the USLSS was active, it is estimated that more than 150,000 people were spared a watery grave. None of this would have been possible had it not been for the vision and tenacity of the earliest members of this organization. What the proverb says is true—without vision the people perish!

Life-Saving Vision

I quickly imagined the parallels between the USLSS and congregations. Purposeful vision was crucial for the effectiveness of the USLSS, and it is equally essential for the local church.

The picture of vision we created in an earlier chapter was that of a line thrown across a rushing stream, anchored to the place we want to be in the future. In this way, vision helps us see where we want to *be*. We as the church can only achieve the vision of where God calls us to *be* when we approach it with the strength of character that comes to us fully anchored in a relationship with God through Jesus Christ and in the power of the Holy Spirit. As I discussed earlier, our operating systems as Christians include repentance and forgiveness, and the outward signs of our character are love—joy, peace, patience, kindness, gentleness, goodness, faithfulness, and self-control. Every congregation's vision of its future can be realized when the whole church is pulling in the same direction. Every community can be transformed by God's power lived out in the church.

I learned in my study of the USLSS that through the vision of one man in particular, Sumner Kimball, the enormous task of ocean rescue became a reality. Kimball was known by all as a man of honor, having been first appointed to the U.S. Treasury Department by President Abraham Lincoln. Those who worked with him over the years found him to be "well-organized, efficient, honest, opposed to special interest manipulation of government agencies, highly intelligent, and deeply caring."[4] Kimball's deepest passion involved lifesaving. Historians write about Kimball: He "understood the sociological fact that dynamic beliefs can motivate people. He believed there was a vital message to spread—that saving lives and property at sea was right and good and that to do so required a first class, paid professional organization of well managed life-savers. These were controversial concepts at the time."[5]

To do what he needed to do, Kimball first hired William D. O'Connor as his assistant. O'Connor was already well established as a first-rate journalist of deep character. His job was to write the stories of the life-saving stations and the vivid accounts of the rescues that were accomplished. Because of his contribution, the stations received the recognition and support they needed from elected officials and the public in order to continue.[6]

Another man of great vision regarding lifesaving was Captain Joshua James. James was appointed keeper of the U.S. Life-Saving Station at Point Allerton in Massachusetts in 1889. In the course of his thirteen-year service there, more than 540 lives and an estimated $1,203,435 worth of ships and cargo were saved.[7] The stories of this man's leadership in the face of adversity are tremendous, but it was his caring attitude toward others that characterized him most. When James was faced with the rescue of the *Gertrude Abbott* in 1888 during a raging hurricane, he told his crew that only volunteers would be allowed to go to the ship for the rescue, because the conditions were so severe that they probably would not return alive. All the men of his crew stepped forward to volunteer.[8]

On March 17, 1902, all but one of the entire crew of the nearby Monomoy Point Life-Saving Station had perished in a rescue attempt. Deeply affected by this tragedy, Captain Joshua James felt it was necessary to step up the rigorous training of his own crew. At seven o'clock on the morning of March 19, with a northeast gale blowing, he called his crew for a drill. For more than an hour, the seventy-five-year-old man maneuvered the boat through the boisterous sea. As he landed his boat on the beach, he praised his team for their hard work, sprang onto the wet sand, glanced at the sea and said, "The tide is ebbing," and with those words dropped dead on the beach. "With a lifeboat for a coffin, Joshua was buried, and another lifeboat made of flowers was placed on his grave. His tombstone shows the Massachusetts Humane Society seal and bears the inscription 'Greater love hath no man than this—that a man lay down his life for his friends.'"[9] This monument to a dedicated public servant continues to inspire those who follow in his footsteps.

These three men, Kimball, O'Connor, and James, illustrate for us the dedication and character it takes to make a vision a reality. Throughout the world today we see those dynamic Christian leaders who show us the courage and tenacity needed to build congregations that are reaching out to their communities for Christ. In awe of their megachurches and multiple ministry settings, we church leaders wonder if we can do the same. For all these leaders, yesterday and today, their largest contribution was following a purposeful vision that moved them toward a better world for those around them. As a whole, the church's mandate is to make a difference in this world—by making disciples and sharing God's love throughout.

Life-Saving Discipleship

When I envision a congregation of Christian disciples, I see a group of folks who not only have received training in areas of Bible study and Christian history and spiritual discipline but also have the fundamental desire to continue their quest for deeper spiritual knowledge. They participate in small groups that encourage their faith development and hold them accountable to that development. They know how to do research with Bible tools, such as concordances, atlases, and Bible commentaries. They practice spiritual disciplines, such as prayer, giving, and contemplation of the Scriptures, for their own development. They have the confidence to speak to others about God's continued presence in their lives. And they have the ability to share their spiritual journey in such a way that folks outside the faith are captivated and touched by their story and want to begin a journey with Christ themselves.

The Life-Saving Station personnel had incredible dedication to the jobs they were hired to do, and the pay these men received was miniscule compared to the life investment they made on the job. The stations were positioned based on the number of wrecks that previously occurred in the area, and crews were responsible for patrolling one to four miles of coastline. From sunrise to sunset, a surfman was stationed on the lookout—usually on top of the station building. The beaches were patrolled on foot during difficult weather and at night. Historians tell us:

> Each day that a lifesaver was on duty was spent doing drills. Sumner Kimball [the General Superintendent of the Service] believed that only training and repetition sharpened your lifesaving skills. That belief still exists today with rescue teams. A lifesaver's week began on Monday with training in the Beach Apparatus Drill including the firing of the Lyle Gun. Tuesday was devoted to boat practice, including the righting of surfboats. The crew practiced signal flag techniques on Wednesday and repeated the Beach Apparatus Drill on Thursday. On Friday the crew could be found practicing first aid and rescue breathing techniques. On Saturday, everyone pitched in and cleaned the station and their quarters.[10]

In the event that a shipwreck was spotted, the training paid off. The surfman on lookout or patrol alerted the crew, and the keeper would decide what apparatus would serve them best as they began their work. If the wreck was close enough, the Lyle gun would be loaded and shot toward the ship. This small brass cannon launched a sturdy line toward the ship with the hopes of anchoring a seventeen-pound projectile to the wreck, and then the line could be used to send breeches buoys and lifecars to the rescue. "Breeches buoys" looked like life preservers, but they had a pair of oversized, short-legged canvas pants sewn inside. A person could sit in the pants and be hauled ashore on the established line. A "lifecar" or "surfcar" looked like a small submarine and was attached onto the line like a gondola. A small hatch on the top allowed several survivors to crawl inside, seal the top, and be pushed or pulled to safety.[11] If the ship was farther out in the surf or stuck on a sandbar, the lifeboats were deployed with the surfmen aboard.

A story is told of a young surfman and his keeper standing on the shore looking out onto the wreck. The surfman asked if the keeper thought the rescuers would come back alive. The keeper responded, "The regulations only say we have to go out. They don't say anything about coming back."[12] The eventual motto of the surfmen became just that: "You have to go out, but you don't have to come back."[13]

One of our biggest mistakes as Christians today is that we often see our preparation not as the means to an end but the end itself. I accept Christ as Savior so that I can go to heaven, I study the Bible so that I can know more about God's activity throughout history, I pray so that I can feel close to God, I go to church so that I can get recharged for my week. The surfmen practiced their skills so that they could go out into the terrifying seas to bring others to safety. Imagine what might happen if we saw our preparation as making ourselves ready to help others deal with life in a world gone mad.

Imagine if people like these surfmen populated our churches. The church of today needs folks who are dedicated to practicing their Christian walk on a daily basis. The church needs folks who are always on the lookout for someone who needs to be saved. We need to learn to use our equipment and to be able to deploy it at a moment's notice. People's lives do depend on the church's ability to be there for them—no matter what. The life-saving surfmen rescued people from ships of every nation—commerce vessels, immigrant ships, and probably a few recreational craft. They didn't pay attention to the wealth of the vessel or what loot they could get from it. They only knew they had to go out to save lives, and they were prepared to build bridges of all sorts to do just that.

Life-Saving Bridge Building

Bridges are unique structures. Sometimes they are built to withstand the tests of time and use, other times they can be quite temporary and used a single time. I see the image of a bridge as something that is used to get from point A to point B, usually over treacherous terrain. In the USLSS, the bridge image captures for me the link between catastrophe and safety, often in the form of the Lyle gun's line that linked the ship to the shore and provided a way of transport across dangerous waves. The work of the lookout alerted the crew when it was time to build a bridge.

Gary tells a great story in the bridge-building chapter about a "lookout" in our rural Ohio church who alerted the congregation to the need of a family in the community. The church responded as bridge builders by selling chili and giving the proceeds to the family in need. When the next lookout spotted a need, the congregation's response was squelched when someone asked about how many needs the congregation was expected to meet. In the United States Life-Saving Service, asking that question would have led to immediate termination. The expectation was that every keeper and every surfman would continue to try to save lives for as long as they were able—no questions asked.

The role of the lookout was critical to the work of each Life-Saving Station. Most of the station buildings were constructed with a tower on top, and the surfman on duty was to stand in the tower his entire shift and survey the waters for ships in trouble. Day watch was kept from sunrise to sunset, and if the lookout

could not see from the tower the whole area the station was responsible for patrolling, then he needed to walk the beach, usually
three times a day, at least to the point where he could see to the
end of the station's area. At night and during bad weather, the
beach patrol was crucial. Two surfmen were designated for each
of four night watches. At their appointed time, they started in the
middle of the patrolled area and walked in opposite directions to
watch the sea for shipwrecks.[14]

While the lookout was the one to alert the station that a ship
was in need, the steps that followed showed the true bridge-
building ability of the station's crew. The keeper's job was to
determine what method would be used to save the ship and its
people and cargo. How close the ship was to shore would determine whether they could use the Lyle gun and breeches buoys or
lifecars, or deploy the lifeboats. Once the keeper made the first
decision, everyone rallied to do the necessary work. If the breeches
buoys weren't adequate, then they would send out the lifecar. If
that didn't work, then the lifeboats were sent to the wreck.

Usually the surfmen were exhausted by the time they got to
the ship, but their most difficult work was yet to come. Depending on the type of ship and the severity of its situation, the crew
and passengers were not the most necessarily cooperative. Regular sailors would have been trained for this type of danger, but
passengers were not, and those who panicked made rescue very
difficult. Reports kept at each station provide an interesting look
into the success of most rescue operations, and one historian ob-
serves: "Usually, no matter how high the seas ran or how hard the
wind blew or how cold it was or how crazed the sailors were, the
surfmen managed to rescue all or most of those on board. The
surfmen had a remarkably high success rate, and once they were
on scene, the odds of mariners' survival approached ninety-nine
percent. If the Life-Saving Service couldn't rescue someone, and
at times they couldn't, that person was either in a very horrible
situation or had been incredibly foolish."[15]

Building bridges out into the communities around our churches
is difficult work. It demands that we stay on the lookout for those

in need, give ourselves to rigorous training, and remain steadfast in the task, even when we face obstacles of various kinds. We too easily get discouraged or busy ourselves doing other less important things. So often we listen to those who put up obstacles to our bridge-building attempts and decide it is just too hard to "go out" into the world and risk not being able to come back.

I am imagining a congregation that starts to build bridges with logical community partners, such as schools and community centers, so that they can celebrate some successes and build confidence in bridge building. When that congregation has practiced and trained and celebrated, then it can begin to tackle some of the harder "shipwrecks" in its community. The church does have the strength and the power of the Holy Spirit to make a huge difference in every local community. We just need to get plugged into that power source, so that when we look out and see a need, we have the right resources to meet that need and save some lives.

An intentional ministry of bridge building can bring hope to the world today—the hope that we claim in our relationship with God through Jesus Christ. *This* hope points us God-ward in personal and corporate worship and then outward in selfless acts of love. I imagine a church effective in its outreach to others because it is first grounded in worship.

Life-Saving Worship

Very little was recorded by the USLSS about the personal or communal worship life of the men and their families. Through the photos I found of people in prayer, however, I can only surmise that faith, at least for some, had an impact on their dedication to saving those lost at sea. I would like to think the parallels between the call of the church to seek and save the lost and the surfmen's own calling to rescue the perishing was obvious to them, maybe so much so they didn't find the need to write about it.

For those of us in the church who are dedicated to a vision of generous disciple-making, bridge-building work in this ever-changing world, our worship of God becomes the impetus for all we do. When we as people of faith gather for worship, we enter fully into an awareness that we do not stand alone in that moment but are part of a faith community that encompasses past, present, and future. Worship, as thin space, opens us more fully to God and to our brothers and sisters throughout the world. Worship ought to remind us that we *are* our "brother's keeper," that "no man is an island," that life is to be "one for all and all for one." The relational nature of worship reminds us that we are connected with God; with each other; *and* with all who have lived, are living, and will live in generations to come.

The church, cocreator with God, fails to use its imagination when it perpetuates a worship style that encourages people to relate to God and to each other *but* does not point them back out into the world to serve those beyond its own faith communities in life-giving ways. I have visited many churches that post signs on their doors that read, on one side, "Enter to Worship," and the other, "Depart to Serve." The "Enter to Worship" part is easy for most of us because we usually get something out of it—for us. That "Depart to Serve" thing? It sounds great but is difficult to do when we are so busy living our own lives and working hard to take care of ourselves. It is astounding to know that many people in our churches really do believe that the old familiar adage "God helps those who help themselves" is in the Bible. We fail to be the people God calls us to be when we gather for worship to be "served up" some God and then go back into the routine of our lives, oblivious to the sea of people splashing and flailing all around us, until it is time to be "served up" some God again.

As our family listened that night on the beach to the stories of those who dedicated their lives to the well-being of others, our hearts were lifted to God with a great sense of awe and gratitude. A thin space emerged for us under the canopy of stars that night. We were with God, with each other, and with the men and women who, by their very selfless acts, served God—even if they were unaware of it—by word and deed. It is difficult for me to imagine how the members of the USLSS could demonstrate such extreme generosity without first being open to and connected in some way to the Divine. One of the hallmarks of a vital congregation is how well that congregation connects to God and to each other in worship *and* steps back out into a world of need to give itself away.

Life-Saving Generosity

I learned the most about generosity when Gary worked as a stewardship consultant. For several years he traveled the country working with churches of various sizes and affiliations, helping them understand the spiritual nature of giving. The years he worked in this ministry were interesting for us as a family. He was usually on the road from Monday morning until late Friday afternoon, leaving the boys and me to fend for ourselves during the week. Now, I am a fairly resourceful person, so his being gone was not a hardship, and we were able to set up a good system of messaging with his pager and cell phone. Yet it was often the stories he brought home with him each weekend, many you have just read, that helped me see the value of his work. This also led me to develop my own sense of generosity about sharing him with the people who needed his services.

Understanding generosity in light of the USLSS gives me a taste of what generous living can mean for us today. One of the most fascinating aspects of the United States Life-Saving Stations was that the keeper and his surfmen managed to have normal lives in the face of their most grueling work. First, these men were paid very little. Second, they had impossible responsibilities. Third, many of the stations were in remote areas. While the keeper was allowed to live at the station, the surfmen had to figure out their own housing. Some of the stations were located near towns, but many were not, so the surfmen eventually built their own cottages near the station and provided a place for their families to live. The role of those families living at the station provides such a glimpse into a truly generous life. Again, the reports of the stations provide us with a great look at where generosity went well beyond the job description of a surfman.

> At many stations when the men went out to a rescue, the women, often with their children, prayed for their husband's safety and the rescue of those on the wrecked vessel. Besides praying, the women might build beach fires as signs of hope and to provide warmth as the rescued and their husbands returned ashore. Warm clothing was gathered and coffee and food was prepared. Survivors and surfmen were often in poor condition when they returned to the station and the women's care could be a matter of life or death. Wives of keepers or surfmen were known to rush into the water to save people. In the aftermath of a wreck, a concerned wife might go searching for her surfman husband, find him exhausted on a frozen beach and bring him safely to the station. The women saved more lives than the public ever knew![16]

The Pea Island Life-Saving Station in North Carolina was home to the only all African American crew. On October 11, 1896, during a hurricane, the American schooner *E. S. Newman* ran aground not far from shore. Because of the location of the wreck and the hurricane winds, none of the crew's equipment could reach the ship. The keeper asked for volunteers from his crew to go into the water for the rescue. Lashed to one another and to those on shore, the men waded to the ship and first rescued the ship captain's young daughter and then his wife. When the surfmen came ashore, two more were sent out and the entire ship's crew was rescued.[17] This story gives a whole new meaning to going out two by two (Luke 10:1)!

The USLSS illustrates for us the personal nature of generosity through the stories of individual acts of courage and bravery, but it also illustrates the corporate nature of generosity when a community puts the needs of others above its own. One definition of generosity is "freedom from meanness or smallness of mind or character."[18] How much could the church of Jesus Christ bring hope to this world if we could embrace a generous nature! Generosity—when we are free from our own fears we can open the church to avenues we otherwise might never consider. Just as generosity led the men, women, and children of the USLSS to doing things "normal" people would never do—like working hard for little personal gain, putting their lives in constant danger, suffering disease and the promise of an early death, moving to whatever place best positioned them to save others—generosity can lead the church in places we never intended to be.

The Portable Church as a Life-Saving Station

To be most effective, Life-Saving Stations were placed in close proximity to the areas where shipwrecks were most likely to occur. This way the crew could respond quickly to the needs of those lost at sea and have the greatest chance of saving them. But beaches, by their very nature, tend not to stay in one place. Normal erosion from the sea and wind constantly reshapes the contour of the coast. So, what was close to the sea one year may be farther away the next. The lighthouse on Assateague Island, for example, used to be positioned near the sea, but because of nature's handiwork over the years, the lighthouse is now more than two miles from the surf. Visiting the island today you can't help but wonder why on earth anyone would put a lighthouse so far inland. Because of the ever-changing coastline, many of the life-saving stations were built to be portable. When needed, the crew could literally pick up and move its entire community to a more suitable life-saving place.

Unlike many of the U.S. Life-Saving Stations, churches have historically been built to remain in one place forever *and* to serve one specific segment of the population. When Gary was appointed as student pastor of Riverside Church, in Harrisburg, Pennsylvania, he stepped into an all white, upper-middle-class, elderly congregation in the midst of a predominantly poor African American community. Just three years prior to Gary's arrival the

demography had shifted rapidly as white residents of the neighborhood moved from the city to the suburbs. Cities aren't the only
areas affected by such migration. Many small towns have suffered
drastic economic shifts when strip malls and shopping centers
have sprouted nearby, drawing customers away from the smaller
mom-and-pop shops that once thrived on Main Street. An ensu-
ing population shift from small town to suburb—closer to work
and to shopping—decimated most of these small businesses and
the town churches that once thrived around them. Tens of thousands of such churches around the country, originally planted
near specific "seas" of people they intended to seek and to save for
Christ, are now boarded up or transformed into antique shops,
clubs, or community centers. Among the many reasons for the
demise of these congregations is a failure to navigate the changing tides of their own communities. Churches that remain fixed
and immobile (and I am not only talking about buildings) stand
the greatest chance of perishing in an ever-changing culture. But
churches that can relocate themselves physically or at least launch
new mission and ministry initiatives where the people *are* have a
greater chance of not merely surviving but thriving in a postmodern world.

Many new churches today, like the two congregations Gary and
I have helped to plant, intentionally situate themselves in portable
locations such as schools, community centers, bars, coffee shops,
or banquet halls. This is true partly because of the enormous cost
of buying land and of building construction—especially for an infant congregation. Many of these new churches want to someday
own a piece of land and build their own facility on it. But some of
these new communities of faith embrace their portability not as a
necessary step toward permanence but as an intentional strategy
to remain transportable, fluid, and unencumbered by the tremen-
dous financial burden owning buildings can cause.

In a transient society like ours, portability may allow a congregation to relocate more easily to reach the people it is trying to
serve as the area itself, like the coastline off Assateague, is reshaped
by the culture around it. Relocating a congregation is never an

easy thing—with or without facilities—but relocation is much easier if the church is not anchored to a specific piece of land by its own buildings.

Church planting also offers an opportunity for healthy existing congregations that *are* fixed in one area to extend their ministry to other growing areas. For example, St. Luke's United Methodist Church has extended itself, through HopeSpring, into the western part of Orange County to be in closer proximity to a planned community that will eventually have nearly sixty thousand new residents. HopeSpring's first worship services were held in an elementary school closer to St. Luke's, but now, eighteen months later, the congregation meets in a public middle school seven miles farther to the west and closer to the new housing areas we are trying to reach. By the end of 2008 our plans are to move into a vacant grocery store another three miles down the road. We will remain in that location for at least five years and decide whether it provides the best position for ministry or we need to relocate to a more suitable place. As a church doing ministry in postmodern culture, we believe portability is important.

While every congregation may not be in a position to relocate itself *or* plant a new church, there may be wonderful opportunities to relocate some of its ministries in areas of need. CrossPoint United Methodist Church in Harrisburg, Pennsylvania (www. xpointumc.org), is just such a congregation. As the church grew over the past decade, it expanded facilities and parking to accommodate more of the people it was reaching from the surrounding community. In the past few years the church's leadership felt a calling to extend itself even further—into the city and neighboring countryside—where the presence of a vital church was lacking. CrossPoint now supports two satellite locations as well as its main campus. One satellite is housed in a public school and the other in the facility of a church that closed. With the exception of part-time pastoral support at the satellite locations, the staff of Cross-Point directs the ministries of all three campuses. CrossPoint is one example of a fixed congregation reaching beyond its shores to seek and to save the lost in other locations. Another church I know in western Pennsylvania has likewise extended ministry from its large main campus to two other locations. One of its satellite sites is an inner-city public school that nearly closed because of a loss of funding. This church came alongside the school to provide financial assistance, send volunteers to help the teachers and staff, tutor students after school, and lead worship for the community in the cafeteria on Sunday mornings.

Several years ago St. Luke's United Methodist Church in Orlando, Florida, established a partnership with a public school that remains in an economically depressed area of the city. Through its School of the Arts program, St. Luke's sends volunteers into the school each week to teach dance, drama, and other creative arts. The paid staff members of St. Luke's support a team of lay volunteers who then carry this unique ministry into an area of great need. More than a decade ago St. Luke's established a medical ministry, called Shepherd's Hope, to help the underinsured of central Florida. Multiple clinics now exist through the area where doctors and nurses volunteer their time to assist people in need.

Because of the vision of its leaders, churches like these have extended a lifeline to those in peril and through the generosity of their congregants built a much needed bridge between the church and the wider community. Lives are being saved from disease, hunger, oppression, and pain because good people—God's people—are willing to move out from *where* they are to meet people *as* they are and embrace them with love.

Just Imagine!

It pains me to think of how nonchalantly we often take ourselves and our ministries in the church. I am not sure we really believe that *who* we are and *what* we do is all that important. We don't really believe that the church *is* the hope of the world. We march into worship with glazed eyes and halfhearted enthusiasm, go about our ministries with a sense of indifference, reach out only to those who will fill our coffers and ensure our survival, give up when to the going gets tough, and retreat behind our walls when we become afraid—and there is a great deal to be afraid of in this world of ours. Some people think the church has run its course and become relegated to the place of irrelevance and obsolescence. I don't buy it!

What if we imagine ourselves differently? What if we imagine ourselves being less about ourselves and more about the people God wants to reach through us? What if we take the Great Commission and Great Commandment as more than just good ideas and seize them as biblical directives? What if we really believe Jesus when he said he would never abandon us? That the power of the Holy Spirit would not only sustain but empower us to do the very things Jesus did? Dare we imagine such things? I pray that we can—and will.

Remember the sketchpad and the itchy couch Gary wrote about in the introduction? God has a place for you just like that in the church—a place that stirs up your creative self *and* at the same time makes you feel a little uncomfortable. Close your eyes for a minute. Imagine what your church would be like—*could* be like—if God has his way with you. What would happen if you let your imagination go wild and really trusted God—and yourself—a whole lot more? So, what is stopping you—besides *you*? God is ready to take the next step. The tools you need are already in your head and heart. Go for it! Go with God. Imagine!

Reflection Questions

1. In what ways is your church the hope of the world around you?

2. Name some of the visionary people who have guided, and are guiding, your congregation.

3. What training are you providing the members of your congregation in order for them to be involved in the life-saving

work of Christ in your community? What specific tools are you providing them?

4. When you look out at the community around you, what specific needs do you see? What kinds of bridges can you build to meet people at their place of need?

5. How does your worship encourage people to think about more than themselves and their own personal relationship with God?

6. How generous is your congregation in its missional outreach to seek and to save the lost? Give examples.

7. What is your congregation doing or could it be doing to become more portable in its missional outreach?

8. What has to change in your life, and in your congregation's life, to fulfill the vision God has for you?

Notes

⤳

Chapter 1   The Constant Waves of Change

1. From Lactantius, *De Mort. Pers.*, ch. 48. opera, ed. O. F. Fritzsche II, 288 sq. (Bibl Patr. Ecc. Lat. XI), in *Translations and Reprints from the Original Sources of European History* (Philadelphia: University of Pennsylvania Press [1897?–1907?]), 4:1, 28–30. This text is in the public domain.
2. Jonathan Hill, *Zondervan Handbook to the History of Christianity* (Oxford: Lion Publishing, 2006), 72, 73.
3. Annals of Congress, "A Century of Lawmaking for a New Nation: U.S. Congressional Documents and Debates 1774–1875," The Library of Congress, http://memory.loc.gov/ammem/amlaw/lwac.html.
4. Virginia Historical Society, "15 January 1974: Sunday-closing Laws," On This Day: Legislative Moments in Virginia History, http://www .vahistorical.org/onthisday/11574.htm.
5. Charles C. Haynes, "Eminent Domain: Seize a Church, Build a Mall?" *Gannett News Service*, August 8, 2005, http://www.spokesmanreview .com/breaking/story.asp?ID=4583.
6. Anthony B. Robinson, "It's a Whole New World: An Online Course on Church and Culture in a New Time," Congregational Vitality, http://www.uccvitality.org/index.php?option=com_content&task= view&id=21&Itemid=40.
7. Bill Easum and Tom Bandy, "Postmodern Compared to Modernity," Easum Bandy and Associates, http://easumbandy.com/resources/ faqs/p/postmodern/postmodern_compared_to_modernity/.

Chapter 2   Imagining a Visionary Church

1. Christian Schwartz, *The Three Colors of Love*, NCD Discipleship Resources (St. Charles, IL: ChurchSmart Resources, 2004), 56–57.

2. Robert L. Moore, "Christianity Sparks China's New Cultural Revolution," *Orlando Sentinel*, July 15, 2007.

3. Eric Van Meter, "GEN-X Rising: Church's Future Depends on Asking New Questions," *UM Portal*, August 16, 2007, http://www.umportal.org/article.asp?id=2429.

4. "Practice phase" refers to a period of about six months when Hope-Spring worshiped in a local elementary school once a month. It was "practice" because we were building teams of people to do the morning set up, hospitality, and children's ministry. Once we moved to weekly worship, we had to know how to do all these things and have enough people trained to do them weekly.

5. Bill Hybels, "Vision to Die For," session 1, *The Leadership Summit 2007*, team ed., DVD (Barrington, IL: Willow Creek Association, 2007).

6. Joel Barker, *The Power of Vision* (St. Paul: StarThrower, 1991).

7. Developed by Church Resource Ministries (www.crmleaders.org), "reFocusing" is a process to create safe-place learning communities that develop authentic leaders who seek to be more passionate about the mission of Christ and a harvest of disciples.

8. Scott Maxwell, "'We All Sin': Ex-legislator Rebuilds His Life," *Orlando Sentinel*, October 4, 2007.

9. Kate Naseef, "How Can the Amish Forgive What Seems Unforgivable?" *USA Today*, October 1, 2007, http://www.usatoday.com/news/nation/2007-10-01-amish_N.htm?csp=34&loc=interstitialskip.

Chapter 3   Imagining a Transforming Congregation

1. John Wesley, "Free Grace," Sermon 128, 1872 ed., John Wesley Holiness of Heart and Life, http://gbgm-umc.org/umw/wesley/serm-128.stm.

2. Robert E. Coleman, ed., *Disciplemaking: Training Leaders to Make Disciples* (Wheaton, IL: Billy Graham Center, 1994).

3. Cathy Lynn Grossman, "Shifting Borders of Faith," *USA Today*, February 26, 2008.

4. Edgar Dale, *Audio-Visual Methods in Teaching*, 3rd ed. (New York: Holt, Rinehart, and Winston, 1969), cited at University of Iowa, College of Public Health, http://www.public-health.uiowa.edu/icphp/ed_training/ttt/archive/2002/2002_course_materials/Cone_of_Learning.pdf.

5. Christian A. Schwarz, *Color Your World with Natural Church Development* (St. Charles, IL: ChurchSmart Resources, 2005), 105.

6. Dictionary.com, s.v. "entrust," http://dictionary.reference.com/browse/entrust (accessed December 14, 2007).

Chapter 4 *Imagining a Bridge-Building Community of Faith*

1. U.S. Religious Landscape Survey, Pew Forum on Religion and Public Life, http://religions.pewforum.org/reports.

2. Reggie McNeal, *The Present Future: Six Tough Questions for the Church* (San Francisco: Jossey-Bass, 2003), 11.

3. Kennon L. Callahan, *Effective Church Leadership: Building on the Twelve Keys* (San Francisco: Jossey-Bass, 1997), 3.

4. Peter Storey, *Listening at Golgotha: Jesus' Words from the Cross* (Nashville: Upper Room Books, 2004), 29.

5. Wilbur E. Rees, *$3.00 Worth of God* (Valley Forge, PA: Judson Press, 1971), from Tim Hansel, *When I Relax I Feel Guilty* (Elgin, IL: David C. Cook, 1979), 49, quoted in Charles R. Swindoll, *Improving Your Serve* (New York: Thomas Nelson, 1990), 29.

Chapter 5 *Imagining Worship as Thin Space*

1. St. Augustine, *The Confessions of St. Augustine*, trans. E. M. Blaiklock (Nashville: Thomas Nelson, 1983), 15.

2. "Willow Creek Repents?" Out of Ur: Following God's Call in a New World, ChristianityToday.com, October 18, 2007, http://blog.christianitytoday.com/outofur/archives/2007/10/willow_creek_re.html.

Chapter 6 *Imagining a Generous Church*

1. Dictionary.com, s.v. "generous," http://dictionary.reference.com/.

2. Richard J. Foster, *Celebration of Discipline: The Path to Spiritual Growth* (San Francisco: Harper and Row, 1978), 70, 71.

3. Associated Press, "Americans Give Record $295B to Charity," USA Today, updated June 25, 2007, www.usatoday.com/news/nation/2007-06-25-charitable_N.htm (accessed May 5, 2008).

4. AllBusiness, www.allbusiness.com/halloween-candy-sales (accessed May 6, 2008).
5. "How Much Do Americans Spend on Christmas Gifts Every Year?" Ask Yahoo! December 14, 2005, http://ask.yahoo.com/20051214.html.
6. "The Beauty Business," Economist.com, May 22, 2003, http://www.economist.com/printedition/displayStory.cfm.
7. Associated Press, "Gourmet Offerings Cater to Pampered Pets," April 26, 2006, MSNBC, http://www.msnbc.msn.com/id/12498847/.
8. Frontline, "Gambling Facts and Stats," Easy Money! PBS Online, http://www.pbs.org/wgbh/pages/frontline/shows/gamble/etc/facts.html.
9. Eric Schlosser, "Fast-Food Nation: The True Cost of America's Diet," *Rolling Stone* (USA) 794 (September 3, 1998), http://www.mcspotlight.org/media/press/rollingstone1.html.
10. Jim Sheppard, "The Challenge of the Church," Generis, http://www.generis.com/resources/challenge_of_church.asp.
11. Donna Schaper, "The Art of the Ask: Getting Good at Fundraising," *Congregations* 34, no. 2 (Spring 2008), 27.
12. Foster, *Celebration of Discipline*, 78.
13. "Affluenza, n. a painful, contagious, socially transmitted condition of overload, debt, anxiety and waste resulting from the dogged pursuit of more." John de Graaf, David Wann, and Thomas H. Naylor, *Affluenza: The All-Consuming Epidemic* (San Francisco: Berrett-Koehler, 2005), quoted in Wikipedia, http://en.wikipedia.org/wiki/Affluenza (accessed May 5, 2008).
14. David Steindl-Rast, *The Music of Silence: Entering the Sacred Space of Monastic Experience* (San Francisco: HarperSanFrancisco, 1995), 30.
15. Foster, *Celebration of Discipline*, 77.
16. Sheppard, "Challenge of the Church."
17. Foster, *Celebration of Discipline*, 77.

Chapter 7   Imagining Church as a Life-Saving Station

1. Ralph C. Shanks, Wick York, Lisa Woo Shanks, eds., *The U.S. Life-Saving Service: Heroes, Rescues and Architecture of the Early Coast Guard* (Petaluma, CA: Costano Books, 1996), 7.
2. Ibid., 13.

3. Ibid., 11.

4. Ibid., 8.

5. Ibid., 8, 10.

6. Ibid., 11.

7. United States Coast Guard, http://www.uscg.mil/history/people/Joshua_James.html (accessed April 16, 2008).

8. Shanks, York, and Shanks, *U.S. Life-Saving Service*, 47.

9. United States Coast Guard, http://www.uscg.mil/history/people/Joshua_James.html (accessed April 16, 2008).

10. "Saints in Sou'westers: The U.S. Life-Saving Service," LifeSavingService.org, http://www.lifesavingservice.org/ (accessed April 7, 2008).

11. Shanks, York, and Shanks, *U.S. Life-Saving Service*, 69.

12. Ibid., 32.

13. U.S. Life-Saving Service Heritage Association, http://uslifesavingservice.org/ (accessed April 7, 2008).

14. Shanks, York, and Shanks, *U.S. Life-Saving Service*, 31.

15. Ibid., 34.

16. Ibid., 125.

17. U.S. Coast Guard Historian's Office, United States Coast Guard, http://www.uscg.mil/history/awards/11%20OCT%201896.html (accessed May 16, 2008).

18. Dictionary.com, s.v. "generosity," http://dictionary.reference.com/browse/generosity.